Bisexuality
A Reader and Sourcebook

Bisexuality
A Reader and Sourcebook

Edited by

Thomas Geller

 Times Change PRESS

Printed by workers under union contract.

Third printing

Times Change Press
Editorial office: P. O. Box 1380, Ojai CA 93024
Sales office: c/o Publishers Services, Box 2510, Novato CA 94948

Typesetting, layout, and design work graciously donated by Freddie Baer, without whose assistance this book could not have appeared nearly so soon or as attractively.

Unattributed drawings are by Bill Himelhoch, to whom many thanks.

Library of Congress Cataloging-in-Publication Data

Bisexuality : a reader and sourcebook / edited by Thomas Geller
    p. cm.
  Includes bibliographical references.
  ISBN 0-87810-037-7 (alk. paper)
  1. Bisexuality. 2. Bisexuality—United States. 3. Bisexuality-
-Societies, etc.—Directories. 4. Bisexuality—United States
-Societies, etc.—Directories. I. Geller, Thomas, 1968- .
HQ74.B58 1990
306.76'5—dc20   90-10975

This book, including the cover, is printed on recycled paper.

Times Change Press is a member of Business Partnership for Peace.

Table of Contents

Introduction

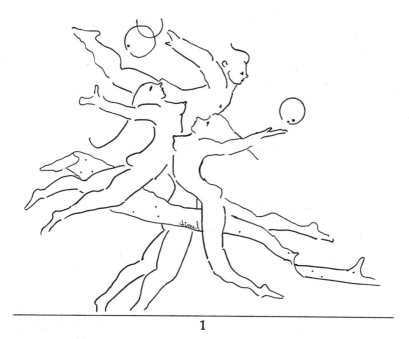

Tidbits!

"Ik eet liever van twee walletjes"
   (Means, approximately, "I like both sides" in Dutch. A button with this expression on it is worn by members of the Werkgroep Bisexualiteit Amsterdam, in The Netherlands.)

Gay Liberation is Our Liberation
"Some folks say that bisexuals are not oppressed because at least we are accepted by mainstream society when we are involved with members of the opposite sex. Agreed, society may like us when we show that piece of who we are. But conditional acceptance is not really acceptance at all. When we show our other side, our gay side, we suffer the same discrimination as other gay men and lesbians. We don't lose only half our children in custody battles. When homophobia hits, we don't get just half fired from our jobs (put on half time, perhaps?). We don't get just half gaybashed when we are out with our same-sex lovers ('Oh please, only hit me on my left side. You see, I'm bisexual!'). We, too, get discriminated against because we are gay."
   Robyn Ochs.

Introduction
By Thomas Geller, Editor

This is my second try at writing this introduction. The first one that I turned into my publisher was full of personal recollections, revelations, and painful remembrances of my emotional and sexual development. Well, he rejected that one as maudlin, embarrassing, and unprintable — and quite rightly so.

But looking at this book in toto and fearing that it might be too textbooklike, clinical, and cold, I feel a need to make an important point here, in the only part of the book I can truly call my own. Bisexuality is only an aspect of some very real, warm, complex, painful, crass, and wonderful lives. As different as those lives are, the existence of bisexuality in people is just as variable, as is its effect and level of importance to the individual. With this in mind, I've tried to keep a balance between the personal type of article and the more technical, academic, or political. And so many of the pieces within are by "just plain (bi) folk" whose only difference is that they thought about how they felt about their sexualities and wrote it down.

I hope to accomplish four things with the distribution of this book: (1) to demystify a subject that is usually only seen in the most sensational of lights ("Man, 37, divorces wife — and marries her brother!" reads one headline), (2) to make sexuality seem less scary and therefore help people deal with their own sexuality by showing that it's really not that big a deal, (3) to put readers in touch with resources by providing the listings found in the last part of this book, and (4) to offer glimpses into the vast and fascinating subject of sexual behavior.

In part, most of my work had already been done for me through the efforts of sexual minorities who were willing to be thoughtful, open, and proud about how their sexuality affected their lives. On this note, I'd like to acknowledge and thank leaders of bisexual, lesbian, gay, transgenderist, and age-, size-, and race-acceptance movements. Each of these communities has built up remarkable resources from which I was able to glean the pieces most relevant to bisexuality for this book. And, throughout my work in compiling it, they've remained helpful, encouraging, and friendly.

With such wonderful resources at my disposal, there are at least three or four pages that I wanted to put in for each one that made it. But Times Change Press, being committed to publishing affordable books, couldn't allow this one to be more than 192 pages without charging more than they felt was accessible. There's still so much material out there; I hope that this book serves as an overview and whets your appetite for more. Here are some of the additional subjects I'd wanted to include but just couldn't here:

- AIDS and sexually transmitted diseases — a guide to recognizing and avoiding them, and how they affect one's view of sex, and society's view of bisexuals

- Bis in marriages and traditional relationships — sociological studies, talks with participants of such relationships, how bisexuality affects monogamy and vice-versa

- Alternative relationships (in greater depth) — triads, polyfidelity, open relationships, sexual friendships, and so on

- Special problems of heterosexual interactions

- Material on other sexual minorities

- Loving contrary to societal standards of race, age, size, and disability

- Starting your own bi support/discussion group

And so many, many other things. Times Change Press hopes that this will prove to be only the first edition of a first book. We may get to some of those other subjects later. And do let us know of any errors, at the address on the copyright page.

Editing this book has made me realize how much outside help

and advice is necessary to do such a project. First and foremost I'd like to thank Lamar Hoover, who was willing to accept the book with only a six-page outline of it from an unproven 20-year-old kid and talk me through two years of self-doubt, incompetence, procrastination, and inexperience. Secondly, I'd like to thank Freddie Baer, layout artist for this volume, for taking my wildly diverse writings and graphics and elegantly converting them — often on an absurdly short notice — into something more nearly resembling a coherent whole.

I'd also like to thank Nikki St. Clair, my good friend and now neighbor. Although you've had nothing to do with this book, Nikki, it couldn't have been done without you. Thank you.

Also high on my gratitude list are: Bill Himelhoch, master of inner peace; Laura Sachs, former editor of *Bi Women* (BBWN) and a truly funny and beautiful woman; Gary North, who has done more to keep people in touch, and against greater odds, than could be expected of anyone; Woody Glenn, of the firm of Glenn, Green, and Hamilton; Robyn Ochs, who's proof that you need not be manic to be successful; Amanda Udis-Kessler, who forgave my transgressions and plays a mean funk keyboard besides; and so many more.

Finally, I'd like to thank the literally hundreds of people who contributed to this book or gave words of encouragement.

A practical note: In order for a book drawn from such diverse sources to have some cohesion, we felt obliged to use a guide to standard editing procedures. We have referred to *The Chicago Manual of Style*, which has been especially useful in establishing some uniformity for the extensive bibliographies (in which, in a few cases, we have substituted an in-print edition we had at hand for an out-of-print one). Interviews have been slightly shortened to avoid repetitions and asides; there have been a few grammatical corrections and some adjustments to allow better placement on the pages. We hope all editing has been light and has not changed any meanings.

Bisexuals
Looking Inward,
Looking Outward

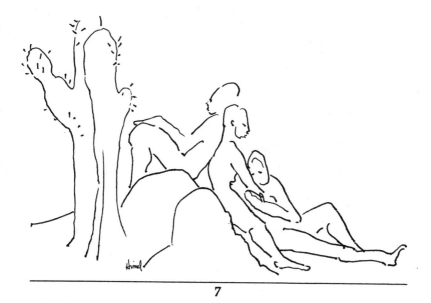

Tidbits!

"Bisexuality is a different way of relating . . . I find I've also become — emotionally speaking — glad to be grey!"
   Tom Robinson *(in* Bisexual Lives*).*

"I'm simply trying to live a both/and life in an either/or world."
   Ibid.

". . . While carnal forthrightness permeates her work, her sexual orientation is the subject of constant debate. She encourages this; she wants everybody to wonder. On The Robin Byrd Show, *Sandra took phone calls from viewers. Male caller: 'What's a guy gotta do to get a date with you? I'm serious.' Sandra: 'Get a sex change!' Female caller: 'What's a girl gotta do to get a date with you?' Sandra: 'Get a sex change!'"*
   The Advocate, *December 20, 1988, quoting an interview by Bill Zehme.*

"Being a bisexual is a lot like being a Tom Waits fan. You grow up thinking you're the only one and not talking about it much. Then when he comes to town, you can't even get a ticket."
   Wayne, The Bi Monthly *(BBMN), November 1987.*

"I have tried everything but necrophilia and coprophilia, and I like kissing best."
   John Waters, film director.

"Two roads diverged in a yellow wood and I, I took both."
   Gary North, editor of Bisexuality: News, Views, and Networking, *altering the poem by Robert Frost.*

An Interview with Robyn Ochs

by Gary North (used with permission of Mr. North and Ms. Ochs)

This originally appeared in the July 27, 1988 issue of Bisexuality: News, Views, and Networking *as part of a larger interview — the other half of which begins on page 40 as "Where the Boys Aren't." In this half, Ms. Ochs talks about her development as a bisexual person.*

Q: How did you first get into the bisexual movement?
A: To start way back, I grew up in a family that was active around antiwar type things, civil rights and so forth. So that's in my blood.
Q: You're how old now?
A: I'll be 30 in October [1988]. When I was a freshman in college — and I was straight all through school to that point — I developed a crush on a woman friend. I thought about it pretty briefly, wrote about it in my journal, and then got involved with a man for two and a half years, which made it a "nonissue."
Q: Did it confuse you at the time? Or did you not think about it?
A: It was very scary. I could not even tell my friend that I had a crush on her. So I acknowledged it, waved at it, and put it away.
Q: How old were you?
A: Eighteen. And then as the relationship with the man started to end, the issue got raised again, because I still had a crush on the same person. So that's when it became a real issue — or a different level of issue. I still wasn't ready to deal with it, though.
Q: I assume that, at the time, you were feministically oriented.
A: Yes, although if there is a difference between knowing something and identifying it with your life, I hadn't made that jump yet.
Q: Did you have any lesbian friends at the time?
A: I had a bunch of lesbian acquaintances. I had one friend who was bisexual. And when I was 23, I got involved with a woman. There were two reasons that I got involved with this person. One was that I had a crush on her, and two was simply that she was a woman, and I knew it was time to act. It wasn't a political decision; it was a decision to grow. And I made a decision to make that frightening jump and to explore that side of myself.

9

Q: At that point, did you also become politically active in regard to bisexuality?

A: Once I got involved with this woman, I was suddenly faced with a lot of issues which I hadn't realized were political, like: why have I assumed all my life that I would be straight and be with a man? Why is it so scary not doing that? Once I started thinking about that, I became more aware of myself — and aware of how afraid lesbians are of coming out or getting help when their jobs can be taken away or they might get beat up. I don't think I was aware of that aspect before then, and this politicized me.

Oh, I should also say that when I was in Connecticut, when I first started to get involved with a woman, I also became aware of how afraid lesbians are of bisexuals, because I was not warmly accepted. I was politely accepted, but not warmly accepted in the lesbian community. I was in a small city. And so there was no organization; there was a social community [instead]. And people were much more polite to me and much more warm toward my lover because she identified as a lesbian and I did not.

When I moved to Boston in 1982, within two weeks of moving here, I participated in the formation of a support group, which was scheduled by the women's center. They had these things called "introductory meetings," and they had rotating topics. The topic, coincidentally, two weeks after I moved here was bisexuality.

At the end of the meeting, two women stood up and suggested that we form a support group, and of the fifteen or so people at that meeting, eight of us formed a support group called the Bivocals. And we met as a support group, and we also encouraged other groups to form, so that by the end of that first year, there were twenty people meeting in three groups. The Bivocals is the group that founded BBWN. That was in 1983.

Q: Why did you decide to pursue this effort to that extent, as compared to just dealing with bisexuality in your own private life?

A: Well, first because I had been raised as an activist. And two of the women in Bivocals were very political women, and it was mostly those two people who brought into the group the political view of not just making your own life comfortable, but of creating something bigger. So Lisa Orlando and Marcia Deihl, who are both very active feminists and both writers and very creative people, kind of planted the bug into the group, and we all caught the fever. It was definitely a group process and definitely collective, but I personally am grateful for their vision.

Q: Had you ever seen yourself as a leader in political terms?

A: I did not see myself as a leader in *any* way. I saw myself as a person who goes to political demonstrations, never the person who organizes them. The first official meeting of the BBWN was facilitated by two other women in Bivocals — I think it was Megan Morrison and Lisa. And I remember sitting there and looking at them with awe and thinking, "My god, I could never do that! I could never facilitate a meeting." You know: "Wow! They must be lucky that they can do that." And I would never place myself in that category. I had no idea that I could ever be like that.

Q: What changed? And when did it change?

A: Well, one thing that changed is the BBWN. It's like I grew up with it, and it was in a lot of ways the instrument through which I grew up: I was at a meeting, and they were short a facilitator for a small group and I was asked to do it and I said, "No way." But there was no one else to do it, so I did it.

Q: How long ago was that?

A: The first year of the BBWN. And so I did it: I ran a group. And I had very mixed feelings about how well I had done, but I did it. And all of a sudden, I said, "Oh. Well, I *can* do it, eh? I might do it *better*, but I can do it." So it was almost as though I fell into the water and found that I could swim, even if I wasn't a good swimmer. So a lot of it was being in the right place at the right time. I also made a decision that year to take chances and to take risks. How do you know you can't do something until you try? Because I had always assumed that I just couldn't do that, I'm just not one of those kinds of people. And I made a decision to try. And, sure enough, I could do it. And as I did it more, I got better at it. And as I got better at it, I had more confidence and was more courageous, and was more creative and consequently did it better. It was a process that built on itself.

Q: In high school or junior high, were you ever involved in student government or anything like that?

A: No. I was in a gospel chorus — just because my friends were. And I was involved in an antidrug program. But I don't think that changed me very much . . . .

Q: Do you have any regrets about being as vocal and open as you have been?

A: First of all, I've situated myself in a position where it's safe to be that. I work in a university that has a nondiscrimination clause, and I live in a city where there's a nondiscrimination clause.

Q: And your family and friends and co-workers?

A: My mother is just fine. She had decided I was bi before I came out to her. And so had my brothers.

Q: Are you the oldest child?

A: Yep.

Q: Out of how many?

A: Three. Two brothers. My mother has a lot of lesbian friends. She occasionally gets uncomfortable when we're excessively lesbiotic [laughs]. She lives up in the country and we've gone to her house with eight lesbians, and my mother — she's cool. She squirms occasionally when we get crazy. But she's as good as she possibly could be, given the generation she grew up in.

My brothers are fine as long as I don't make a big deal out of it in front of their friends. I mean, they're kind of embarrassed. They're supportive, but not comfortable. One of my brothers said, "That's fine, but I would prefer that you didn't talk about it in front of my roommates." Their ages are 24 and 27.

And my father is not pleased. He loves me and he tries to be supportive, but he is not pleased. Because he believes in the One True Way. I mean, speaking from his own experience, he believes that the only true bond is between a man and a woman. So he thinks I'm not being real.

Q: But otherwise he has a liberal, activist background?

A: My father's an armchair radical. My mother's more of an activist. But he's got good politics in general.

Q: How about the people you work with?

A: The staff that I work with are wonderful. It's interesting: out of the group there are two celibate people, two married people, one lesbian, and me. So that sets up an interesting situation: no one's in the majority. Both celibate people are heterosexual, but they're not in relationships nor are they expecting to be. So everyone on the staff I work with is just wonderful, and everybody thinks that everybody else is kind of, you know, — amusing. A little bit strange, maybe.

There was a lot of a stir when I was quoted in *Newsweek*, and I think they were all excited when I was on "Hour Magazine." But the reaction was not "Oh my god, she's a bisexual," but "Oh my god, she's in *Newsweek*!" And the same was true when I did the TV thing. They were excited that I was on TV more than mortified that I was bisexual or something.

Q: So you're something of a celebrity?

A: Yeah, like a pet freak or something [laughs] — but I'm not the only one.

Q: Are you currently in a relationship? With a man or woman?

A: Woman.

Q: And she defines herself as what?

A: Lesbian. The two straight men I was involved with since I came out have both been fine, but they've both been activist-type men, very political. In fact, they marched in the annual Gay Pride march this year. Part of it is traveling in the right communities. I choose for my community people who will not be homophobic and people who accept me for who I am. My current lover marched with the bisexual contingent at The March on Washington for Gay and Lesbian Rights in 1987. We weren't lovers at the time yet, but she marched with me, which I felt was the strongest thing she could have said to me, because a lot of lesbians would be afraid to do that; they'd be afraid people would think they're bisexual.

There are many lesbians who are biphobic, and there are many who are not. Organizationally, the Boston gay papers have been increasingly supportive of bisexuality. We've been getting media coverage. They acknowledge that we're out there, and I think that the reception has been increasingly welcoming.

Bis and Androgyny Today
by Gary North

This article originally appeared in the September 19, 1988 issue of Bisexuality: News, Views, and Networking. *Used with permission.*

Can you imagine what Michael Jackson's resumé would look like if he were applying for a "regular" job in the "real" world?

What does a former member of Poison, Def Leppard, White Lion, Motley Crüe or Ratt do once he (?) retires from heavy metal?

Where do you go after you've played with a group called AC/DC, Iron Maiden, Queensryche, Kiss or Brunette (an all-male group vamping up as rockers from hell, the kind of guy their moms did *not* want them to know, let alone be attracted to or grow up to be!)?

How is it that these drag-queen/macho-man/crazed-rocker/sensitive-guy hybrids are popular modern heroes?

And why are they almost exclusively seen as straight? (And, it seems almost equally true, they *are* straight.)

What does all this say about bisexuality and androgyny in today's North American culture?

Perhaps the media's and public's lack of response is ignorance, avoidance, or both. Perhaps that could explain why no one seemed to bat an eye when pop star Madonna went on David Letterman's show and dropped bombshells all over the stage about an affair she may have been having with another woman.

When I asked a very straight 13-year-old family friend why his favorite heavy-metal rock stars dress like women, he said, "That's how they dress" — as if it were some sort of requirement among such performers to wear long hair with bangs, lipstick, huge earrings, and glitz to the max.

It all seems to hark back to the 1950s and '60s and before, but with a new twist. Come with us now to the bygone years when:

Flappers and the jitterbug alarmed America — women throwing their legs around men, looking like they were having sex.

What Elvis did with his pelvis on Ed Sullivan's TV show wasn't what men did in public, let alone what women did anywhere.

The Beatles brought long hair to the States, and nothing has ever been the same.

So perhaps it is not a surprise that from the antics of the late (and not-so-great) Kabukilike Kiss to the painted nonladies of today's rock stars, no one is labeled as gay or bi. Well, lots of folks have wondered if his royal badness, Prince, is bi, but I doubt it; narcissistic perhaps, but where would he get the time to do anything anyway — he is always producing or writing something. (Of course, it could be argued that narcissism is a form of homosexuality, especially if one achieves orgasm.) And then there's Mr. Bad himself, Michael J., but who cares when you dance like that? Still, these are today's American cultural heroes, the ones that young boys enjoy watching; they might not want to *be* like them, but they have no fears of being called queer for liking them.

And then there's Heart and Pat Benatar and Joan Jett. (And let's not again fight the battle over who gets Holly Near, O.K.?)

In the case of our rock stars, girls can be girlish to the point of being slutty (Madonna and Cyndi Lauper), and boys can be girlish to the point of — well, apparently not so far that people begin to wonder. Listen to their lyrics, listen to them talk: those guys are pretty, but they're also pretty much straight — almost chauvinistic. (The weird thing is: what kind of straight woman would be attracted to one of these guys? Would that be a sign of *her* gayness?)

A friend of mine says it all began in the rebellious Vietnam War era, when the kids grew their hair long or frizzy to break from tradition and their parents' ways. That rebelliousness became something of the norm, and now we're back to short hair for the popular heroes, except for heavy metallists and a few others. Yeah, yeah, I know Bruce Springsteen has short hair, and yeah, once upon a time David Bowie and Elton John decided they were bi and then got married and continued to play it straight, or said that their consciousness was their musicality, not their sexuality, and they wear short (straight?) hair these days, too.

So where are we now? Androgyny or cross-dressing or something approaching heavy-metal camp is in, but bisexuality is not chic — not in this age of AIDS. Where does that leave us?

Back up a bit. The issue is androgyny. That means having looks or affectations or sensitivities and sensibilities common to both males and females. Androgyny is not the same as bisexuality. Bisexuality means having the capacity to be *attracted* to people of both major genders (don't forget: there are gender minorities, too). Androgyny, for our purposes here, means *having characteristics common to both genders.* So just because some guy looks like a "queen" or is "effeminate" doesn't mean he is gay or bi.

But this is Ronald Reagan's America, or at least a good part of it is. If one of those guys decided to become a stock broker or middle manager, he'd have to cut his hair. Eyeliner and lipstick were never popular for men in this century except in a few bars, on Milton Berle in drag, and now on some rock stars. What does that say?

Must a man be androgynous to be bi? Should he be? Should a woman be more "manly?" One bi woman I know says she becomes more feminine around women and more boyish or manly around men. Another bi woman I know experiences just the opposite: she feels she's more "manly" around women and more "womanly" around men; she likes to be "the little woman" with guys (usually they are taller than she is), but takes charge when she's in relationships with gals. Others I know of don't perceive a change in their behavior, demeanor, or looks. Historically, I get gentler around women and, depending on the guy, sort of a toughy (don't show my emotions, be manly) until I feel more comfortable around him, and then I get sort of wacky or boyish; eventually my behavior evens out, and I'm the same with both men and women — alternately gentle, quiet and kidlike (when we're not arguing or breaking up; then I take my marbles and go home).

I'd like to explore androgyny as it relates to our *behavior* as bisexual people: the way we dress, the way we act, and so forth. For some, it's a nonsubject. For others, it's a part of the coming-out process: a releasing of that personality they've kept closeted all these years because they were afraid it would "give them away." And in all cases, the issues are linked to culture and nation, so what is bi or androgynous in the U.S. or Canada might not be seen as such in, say, Mexico or Africa.

Just because I'm bisexual don't assume I'm a slag!
by "Vi"

This article was originally published in the (London) Bi-Monthly *("The Magazine for Bisexuals"), Issue 20, October 1988, page 19. Used with permission.*

I've been amazed to receive letters from men who read *Bi-Monthly* who seem to assume that because I'm bisexual then I must be a slag.

The offers I have been made in recent months have amazed and saddened me, and sometimes made me laugh. Some assume I'll be into group sex, some take it for granted I'll take up any offer of sex, regardless of who it was that was offering it. Some have asked my girlfriend and myself to be part of a fantasy of theirs, along the lines of a bedroom scene show. The reality is far from all these fantasies, sorry to disappoint you folks!

I'm not into group sex, threesomes or foursomes! My sexual life is a very private part of my life, so I'm not going to answer letters along the lines of what I like in bed, or even who I like to go to bed with. I'm actually married, so I'm not interested in other men purely for sex.

It's no wonder with some of their attitudes that they are not successful in their relationships.

One letter read, "I know you are bisexual, so you will know what I am after, to have sex."

Personally I believe that to have a good sexual relationship, a loving relationship is also needed. But some of the letter writers assume I don't have feelings.

Please don't assume that because I'm bisexual it must mean I'm into a whole host of weird and kinky situations.

Don't assume because I'm bisexual I must be a slag!

(Editor's note: According to my research, slag, which literally means slack, is British slang for a loose person or "swinger.")

The Transgend-Dance
by Andy Plumb

Originally published in the December 12, 1988 issue of Bisexuality: News, Views, and Networking, *as part two in the continuing series "Bis and Androgyny Today." Used with permission.*

Every few years I get this compulsion to redefine my sexuality; to come up with an identity to play with until it bores me, turns into a self-cliché, or I metamorphose into something different. I've been a bisexual-transvestite, a quadrisexual, a male lesbian, an androgyne, a "Don't label me"/post-modern sexual being, and though I wonder about the connotations of "polymorphous perversity," it may be as apt a description of my sexuality as I've ever taken on.

Last night, as I madly switched television channels from 2 to 36 and back to 2 again, I came to the realization that as of my 37th birthday, August 31, 1988, I'm a Bi-Bi Sexual (which doesn't mean I'm saying bye-bye to sex, though my few and far between erotic experiences beyond self-pleasuring the past three years might lead one to that conclusion). Let me explain. You see, in my "normal" day-to-day presentation of self to the outside world, I'm Andy: a youthful-looking (most people assume I am in my mid-20's) male who is attracted to and has played passionately with men and women. But through the looking glass dwells my persona/feminine entity/Anima (who I named Selena Anne about seven years ago), who has also enjoyed erotic pleasure with members of both genders of the human species. (Some of the men were also playing out their feminine fantasies).

I was nine years old when *she* came into my life. I have no recollection of ever consciously asking for her; she just appeared, in the guise of a silky slip. The moment I first dropped the compelling garment over my head, letting it slide down my pre-pubescent body, I was awakened to an intoxicating world of the senses that I had been unaware of previously. While dressed in my mother's or sister's clothes, I was able temporarily to transcend what I considered to be the difficult, frustrating trials and tribulations of boy-hood: the fights over whether I was safe or out, the hiding of my tears from friends, the continual striving to be the best math student or fastest runner or class clown. Much to my displeasure, my feelings of ecstasy would be overtaken by paranoia, guilt, and extreme loneliness.

Despite the seemingly miraculous powers of fashions deemed "for women only," I had few longings to leap from my birthgiven male gender to female. I think that if I had had my druthers — if some superpower could have granted my wish — I would have chosen to live happily as a baseball-hurling, panty-clad, outside-the-boundaries-of-the-either/or boy/girl. (That still sounds nice.) But given the extreme gender stereotyping and trapping that dominated life in mid-twentieth-century America, I had little faith that my idealistic dreams would ever be realized.

I had my first boy-to-boy sexual experience with Michael[1], who lived across the street. I still am able to conjure up images of him stroking my turned-on penis while singing Beatles songs ("I Want to Hold Your Hand," "When I Saw Her Standing There," etc.). I couldn't get enough of his attention, and was very upset when his family took his hand out of my life, by moving out of the area. Luckily, I found a couple of other friends to goose around with. Charles, the very "straight and narrow" boy next door, pulled a nice surprise one sleepover evening by climbing on top of me and simulating intercourse. On another night together, I got real brave and shared my secret world with him. Not only wasn't he bothered but he joined me in the wearing of frilly panties, bras, stockings and other pieces of feminine finery (I have this sneaking suspicion that he now wears his wife's undergarments beneath his corporate uniform). One other friend and I did the transgend-dance a couple of times, but that period of innocent exploration had to come to an end, alas.

During my freshman year of high school, I found myself des-perately yearning for a capital G Girlfriend (someone to kiss be-

---

[1] *All names of sexual partners have been changed.*

hind the Ferris wheel at the local Walnut Festival), while trying to deny my interest in boys, fearful I might get labeled "queer." Despite my desires, I was so shy with girls that I did not even go on a date until I was a senior, and even then I didn't have the nerve to kiss any of them goodnight. Consequently, Selena Anne and I became more and more intimate during my high school days. We were an intense on-again/off-again couple (I loved her, I hated her, she could take me to the heavens and down to hell in an hour or two).

When I went away to college, instead of diving into "the sexual revolution" (late 1960s), I retreated further into myself, unsure of where to go or what I wanted to be. I would occasionally have fantasies of men exciting me in ways that my childhood playmates had done (I was fairly sure that gay sex was not just a phase I had gone through), but these were rudely expelled from my mind when a rather stoned man mistook my 19-year-old friendliness for a sexual come-on. It took me years to get over the frightening image of his clammy hands grabbing my throat.

If I didn't have my Selena Anne persona to metamorphose into, I'm not sure I would ever have been able to express my Andy-self with a male. She provided a buffer, a pretense at heterosexuality. When in drag, I knew I wasn't the real thing — a genuine gal — but I made a damn good facsimile, and found it a lark to be exploring the "forbidden territory" outside the gender lines with another person. (Most of the men I've been with while I was dressed in women's clothes would identify themselves as "straight," despite evidence to the contrary.)

In relating to genuine women, I lacked confidence to the tenth degree (I would aim for massage parlors when I could no longer hold back my horniness). At the age of 23, I finally found the Girlfriend I'd been madly desiring for a decade. I went from a singular identity to "Andy and Nancy" almost overnight. We spent every moment together (or so it seemed), usually in bed, trying out Kama Sutra positions one through thirty-seven. I put Selena in my dorm closet, not knowing how Nancy would react to this aspect of me. Just at the point when I felt ready to open up to Nancy, she said "sayonara," which made the breakup even more difficult to deal with.

When my second love, Alaina, accidentally (?) came across a drawerful of black corsets, garter belts, and other clues to my wild side, I expected her to leave me in an instant, but instead she was intrigued by Selena — more so than she was by my revealed Andy persona. For the next few months we played dress-up (as a "tomboy," she had avoided girlish clothes in earlier days) and explored an alternative sexual fantasy/reality. Selena and I were thrilled to finally be playing with a flesh-and-blood woman; it was almost as much fun as the scintillating scenes that had reeled through my mind. If only Alaina and I had jelled in other ways, if only . . . .

A few years later I got involved with Elly, a young, artistic woman who had become encrushed by a punkish Selena (clad in black fishnets and bright red vinyl miniskirt) at a Halloween party. For nearly a year, we lustfully performed the transgend-dance, taking it into realms that went beyond my wildest imaginings. (We had tried heterosexual, naked-male-body-to-naked-female-body sex a few times, but it was unsatisfying to both of us). Elly liked to take on a more masculine/dominant role that was mindblowing, scary, and exciting at the same time. We also engaged in a few *ménages à trois* with members of either gender. Eventually, Elly's passion for Selena waned (I wanted to take us even further into forbidden territory) and she ran off to live with a real woman in San Francisco. It seems that playing girl with Selena was a steppingstone to lesbianism, which Elly now wholeheartedly embraces.

In the past four and a half years, I have had a few short-term affairs with women (two of who enjoyed playing with Selena, while one wanted her to remain in the closet), and assorted safe sex experiences with men (occasionally as Selena, usually as Andy), but most of the time it's been just the two of us behind closed doors. I've come to accept, appreciate, understand, and love my feminine entity (in her many personifications) more often than not, which is a great improvement from earlier times. I've found myself playing "girl" on days when I wake up singing, "Oh what a beautiful morning," as well as on my "To be or not to be" days.

When Selena and I are on, I wonder why I waste any energy "a wishing and a hoping" for a lover, feeling that she or he would have to be extraspecial to top our passion. Still, I do yearn for more connection and only hope that when Mr. or Ms. As Right As One Can Be These Days comes along, that he or she will not only tolerate Selena, but will revel in her.

On one level, I'm aware that Selena's only a closetful of clothes, just a material girl at best, a stereotypical female being without substance; on the other hand, rolling on a pair of black lace stockings, draping myself in a satin slip, and stepping into 4-inch spiked heels rips apart the masculine straightjacket that usually engulfs me; I feel an energy, a vibrancy, a sense of self that I've never experienced encased in a three-piece-suit or in Levi blues and a T-shirt. Ironically, I oftentimes feel more powerful when I am impersonating a woman than when I impersonate a man. I do not believe I am feasting on negative images of women (which some feminists have said of transvestism), but that I am working/playing towards the end of gender fascism. It all really comes down to: who should be the boss — you or your gender?

Reflecting on Physical Disability and (Bi)sexuality
by Pamela Walker

This originally appeared in the July 1987 issue of Bi-Lines *(Pacific Center), entitled "Reflecting on Disability and Bisexuality." Used with permission.*

The July 1987 issue of *Playboy* features a disabled woman, Ellen Stohl, in one of its pictorial spreads (pun intended). It seems some people (mostly nondisabled) feel it is in poor taste to show a disabled woman in this way. I realize that the issue of exploitation is a concern, but many people who generally accept *Playboy* as O.K. are upset because the woman is disabled. Whether they are reacting out of protection, guilt, shame, or revulsion, I find the reaction inappropriate. People feel a variety of ways about *Playboy* modeling (i.e. trash, erotic art, etc.) and, ideally, one's view of that kind of role would remain unchanged by the fact that a model is disabled.

I think it's rather exciting — it's about time for the world to realize that disabled people can be sexy also. The issue of whether or not these magazines exploit women has dropped right into the disabled community; there is finally a recognition that we are sexual beings. These things show progress. I also felt it was progress the first time a physically disabled athlete was featured on a cereal box. Regardless of the circumstance that it was a male in the athletic role, while the female gets the cheesecake role, I still think it's exciting. I feel that one of the hardest things disabled people face is being seen as sexless by a society that places a high value on sexuality. Ellen Stohl has thrown a bomb at, or at least taken a chisel to, that stereotype. (A part of this issue is sexual attractiveness, but it is even more than that: many people who are seen as unattractive by our social standards are still seen as sexually functional; however, disabled people are seen as nonsexual regardless of whether or not they meet other criteria of attractiveness.)

I am a 38-year-old disabled woman who refuses to accept the "sexless" label. My disability is the result of polio; I use a power wheelchair and have limited use of my arms. I've been disabled most of my life; I learned about stereotyping long ago. My disability is obvious, so my label is visible. "Coming Out" as a bisexual was taking a hidden label, wearing it on the outside, and learning to wear it with pride. I think it was easier since I'd already learned how to survive with an obvious label.

Well, maybe it was *easier*, but it still wasn't *easy*. . . .

A family that cheers for a disabled sister/daughter/niece doesn't want to hear that she sleeps with women. People already feel she's got enough going on to make her life difficult — why can't she just find a nice protective man and be happy?

And of course acquaintances and coworkers have their version of why she turned to women — it has to do with misconceptions about her not being able to satisfy a man or have normal sex. In fact, many times it's even "understandable"; at least now she has a companion. Although this makes it easier to have female lovers treated respectfully, it stinks so badly of deprecation that I'd rather have the suggestive gossip. (Ah! Fond memories come to mind of the lovely nurse that I went out with. No one ever suspected a thing.)

The thought that it's "understandable that a disabled woman would turn to a woman since she can't please a man" is full of distortions. The concept implies that there is less need for her to "please a woman." Is that because our society has put so much emphasis on the man being the one who gets pleasured? Also implied is that a disabled woman can't please a man. I think my male lovers would dispute that without any coaxing! I actually have more doubts about satisfying women than I have about satisfying men, because of my weak arms and shoulders. (At the risk of being censored, let me just say that I can always do O.K. with a man: even when my hands wear out, the legs still spread.) However, experience has shown me that this fear of inadequacy is groundless. I am sure my female lovers would also give me satisfactory letters of reference!

Often I'm asked if I find men and women treat me differently regarding my disability. Speaking only for myself, I would say: *yes*. Women have been less likely than men to see me as a potential sexual partner; all the talk about including disabled sisters in the movement usually doesn't extend to the bars and the social scenes. However, those women who have been intimate with me have generally treated me more naturally and equally than the men who have been intimate with me. I have had lovers who idolized me, lovers who over-protected me, lovers who have fulfilled their need to be needed with me, and other trips that were exaggerated by my disability. But, for the most part, those have been male lovers. In summary, men are wonderful for casual or short-term relationships; women, though less likely to get involved with me, come closer to meeting my idea of what love and relationships are all about. It's important to note, though, that there have been exceptions to these generalizations in my relationships with both men and women.

To write about disability is a subject that could spin off in so many directions. In some ways bisexuals are all the same and in other ways they are all different; disability is one of those differences. But we all fight the same battle of nonexistence: the idea that there is no such thing as a bisexual. (There are straights who are playing around and gays and lesbians who occasionally detour, but there are no bisexuals . . . and none of them is disabled.) I'm the only visibly disabled, openly bisexual person that I know. I am sure that the number of disabled bisexuals is very high; however, either the disability is hidden or the bisexuality is hidden, or both. Therefore, it is vitally important that bisexual support systems be physically accessible (ramps, room enough for wheelchairs), environmentally accessible (no perfumes or smoke), language accessible (sign language interpreters), material accessible (large print, tape), and attitudinally accessible (understanding physical, emotional, and mental disabilities). It is unreasonable to expect that all of this will happen overnight, but movement in this direction is important; and it is important to include disabled people in on the process.

Sensually yours, Pam Walker

The Best of Both Worlds and Still Nothing:
Bisexuals Come Out to Talk
By Melinda Wittstock

This article was carried by the Canadian University Press' special Lesbian and Gay Feature Exchange, and appeared in the May 1987 issue of Rites, a lesbian and gay magazine with a feminist bent and with a commitment to progressive social change. (Ten issues per year for $16 (Canadian); U.S.A. and Overseas: $18. Write to: Box 65, Station F, Toronto, Ontario, Canada, M4Y 2L4.)© 1987.

Bisexuality. To many, the word conjures up an image of a decadent, wishy-washy, fence-sitter, unable to find his or her "real" sexuality. To many, real bisexuality doesn't even exist.

Either bisexuals are seen to be going through a "phase" of experimentation before heading back to straightsville, or they're just in the process of coming out as lesbians or gay men. At the same time, bisexuals often experience the same prejudice and discrimination from the straight community as do lesbians and gay men, although many lesbians and gay men are quick to label bisexuals as privileged — they can cling to the legitimacy of a straight relationship while being able to enjoy the benefits of loving members of the same sex. Bisexuals are not fully accepted by either community, nor do they have a community or identity of their own.

It's not surprising that few bisexual women and men assume a bisexual identity. Many bisexuals choose to integrate themselves into either the homosexual or the heterosexual community, while others fluctuate between the two communities in different social contexts or periods of their lives, changing labels when appropriate. Rarely do bisexuals seek a sexual identity separate from lesbians and gays, or straights. But more and more bisexual women and men are speaking out about the discrimination they suffer at the hands of both "established" sexual communities. "I think we are a group like any other," says Jeannie Corrigal, a student at Concordia University in Montreal who recently founded a group for bisexual women called Bifocal. "But I'm tired of being told that we have 'the best of both worlds' or, worse still, that we don't exist."

Corrigal says it took her a long time to be able to talk about her bisexuality. "It wastes more time and energy being guilty about something you shouldn't have to be guilty about," she says. "It's such a relief to talk about it."

Madeleine Byrnes, a Toronto feminist, came out as a bisexual during a workshop she had coordinated for a women's sexuality conference in Toronto just over a year ago. "At the workshop I gave, I was stunned by the number of bisexual women in the closet and how much we all have in common."

"I had had this love affair with another woman, but I had thought that unless I could be sure I'd be involved with another woman again, I couldn't call myself bisexual," said Byrnes. But she soon found she wasn't alone: many women in the group said they felt the same way. The women also talked about the pressures both communities put on bisexuals to choose between either a strictly lesbian or a straight lifestyle. "All of this and more came out at the workshop and we realized there were lots of us. That's when I came out."

Alan Love, a coordinator of a men's consciousness-raising group called the Toronto Men's Forum, says he wants to start up "some sort of support group for bisexual men in Toronto." Love gave a workshop on male sexuality with two other men — one straight, the other gay — at a Kingston, Ontario men's conference in October 1986. He says there were a surprising number of men that wanted to discuss bisexuality. "Many said they had a need for a support group for bisexual men — there was a lot of support for it," he says.

"I want the bisexual community to have a strong and clear voice," says Love, who is also involved in starting up a new magazine called *Integral* for men of all sexual orientations. "Bisexuals have been invisible for too long."

But the political and cultural necessity of exclusive homosexual identification, for the sake of gay and lesbian visibility in a society where heterosexuality is virtually compulsory, has polarized human sexuality. Bisexuality is excluded, but not because it doesn't exist.

"Our culture has identified with heterosexuality for centuries, but the success of gay liberation in launching a very visible attack on a homophobic society has meant there are now two official sexualities, two separate ethics," says Jean Francois Renaud, an Ottawa DJ and waiter who is bisexual. "And society, at one point or another, forces you to make an exclusive choice between the two."

Alfred Kinsey, well-known sexuality researcher and author, believed this enforced polarity is unnatural. "The world is not to be divided into sheep and goats. Not all things are black nor are all things white. It is a fundamental taxonomy that nature rarely deals with discrete categories and tries to force facts into separate pigeonholes," wrote Kinsey in his 1948 book Sexual Behavior in the Human Male. "The sooner we learn this concerning human sexual behavior, the sooner we shall reach a sound understanding of the realities of sex."

Kinsey rated human sexuality on a scale of zero to six. Homosexuality never even crosses into the minds of number zeroes, said Kinsey, while number sixes pretty much know they are completely gay or lesbian the moment they're born. Kinsey posited that most people fit in somewhere between one and five — only five percent of the population, he wrote, live at either extreme. Lesbians occasionally have sex with men; gay men occasionally have sex with women. And most avowed heterosexuals have had at least one homosexual experience during their lives, Kinsey's research indicates.

But though bisexuality may in fact be the "true" sexuality of the majority of the population, it still doesn't mean it is socially acceptable. Most heterosexuals are quick to express their hatred and fear of love and affection between members of the same sex, whether those engaged in homosexual relationships define themselves as bisexual or homosexual.

But at the same time, bisexuality is seen as a threat by many in the homosexual community, given the systematic attempts of a homophobic culture to "cure" gays and lesbians of their "malady."

"Lesbians often feel threatened by bisexual women because there's so little security within the lesbian community, so little support for lesbians, and such strong pressure from the so-called heterosexual world to make lesbians become straight, that lesbians' getting involved with men seems to undermine any security we may have," says Maggie de Vries, a graduate of the University of British Columbia who is now a full-time activist in both the lesbian and feminist movements in Montreal.

Lesbian separatism as a political alternative to a male-dominated society has precluded the possibility of bisexual women's participating in some lesbian communities or organizations. Luba Szkambara, a student at Carleton University who recently came out as a bisexual, says lesbians "see bisexual women as opting for a male-centered society and the patriarchy whenever [they] sleep with a man."

But Szkambara says her politics don't dictate who she sleeps with. "I don't sleep with men for acceptance from male society nor do I sleep with women as a part of a rebellion from that society. For me, desire cannot be determined by politics."

Jenny Beeman, an active member of McGill University's Women's Union, says the "pressure from the lesbian community not to define yourself as bisexual is more overt than from the straight community. You get things like 'we don't know if we want to work with you' if you're out as a bisexual woman."

But Byrnes says the feminist movement must become more open to bisexual women. "The feminist movement," she says, "is like one big family, where everyone has in common a passionate commitment to the liberation of women. But the biggest issue in any family is 'am I allowed to be different and still be loved?' In the feminist community, this question comes up around class, women of color and sexual preference. I think the issue is the right to be different and still be connected."

Although bisexual women "need support from lesbians because they certainly aren't getting any from the straight community," says de Vries, "there are times when lesbians need to work with other lesbians only."

De Vries points out that "any oppressed group experiences distrust with any group that is not fully part of that oppressed group. Bisexuals," she says, "don't always recognize this or their relative privilege."

Mary Louise Adams, a lesbian feminist and member of the Toronto-based lesbian and gay *Rites* magazine collective, says bisexual women can cling to straightness for the benefit of their families or jobs. "Although a bisexual woman going out with another woman gets the same oppression as a lesbian, it's important to keep in mind that too many bisexual women save their public, long-term relationships for men and their private affairs for women."

"It's not that lesbians generally discount the existence of bisexuality," says Adams. "It's just that lots of lesbians have been burned by bisexual women. And when the heat is on, they often go back to men."

But many bisexual women say they don't think they are any more privileged than lesbians. "Bisexual women aren't more privileged," says Paula Siepniewicz, a feminist who is officially "out" as a lesbian to both communities, but tells only her close friends about her bisexuality. "With all the hassles bisexuals have to deal with, it probably equals out."

Siepniewicz, a philosophy student at the Université de Montréal, says her oppression as a woman is much clearer to her than her oppression as a lesbian. "Bisexual women lead more difficult lives," she says. "Because lesbians live their lives in such closed space, they don't have to deal with sexist oppression as much as bisexual women because they refuse to have anything to do with men."

Bisexuals are put in the position of having the best of both worlds and still nothing. They "may open themselves to greater experience," says Renaud, "but when they inevitably suffer the same discrimination as lesbians and gay men, there's no support network, no community to turn to."

As Siepniewicz points out, "it's already hard to come out as a lesbian. But for bisexuals, it's like coming out in a desert. For the time and energy that it takes, I often think it's not worth explaining my bisexuality to people."

Love says he avoids going out with men who are strictly gay because he gets "this 'you're confused' line, you know, the 'you're really one of us; you really want to suck cock for the rest of your life' kind of thing." He says he gets told bisexuality is "trendy" and that he's just trying to fit in. "Others say, 'well, it was in a few years ago,' in the same way they'd say, 'well, sushi was in a few years ago; but now it's Vietnamese or Korean.'"

"I get put off by all of that," says Love. "I'm not gay and I'm not heterosexual. I'm bisexual. I look at myself as a sexual person — sometimes with women, sometimes with men — that's just me."

Thomas Burnside, a Montreal gay activist and co-coordinator of Lesbian and Gay Friends of Concordia (LGFC), says many lesbians and gay men assume bisexuality is "just a coming-out phase because they went through a bisexual phase themselves."

"Gay men who had trouble dealing with their feelings for other men and slept with women to deal with their insecurities," says Burnside, "probably think many of the bisexual men they run into are going through the same thing. For this reason, some gay men think that bisexuality doesn't exist — that it's merely a refusal to be honest about one's sexuality."

Faced with this kind of judgment, bisexuals can respond in one of three ways: they can be "honest" and acknowledge their "true" homosexual preference; they can revert to heterosexuality and reveal their bisexual activity to have been nothing more than experimentation; or finally, they can retain a bisexual identity and remain "dishonest."

Many bisexuals say they've had enough of both the heterosexual and homosexual communities trying to force them to pick a side and stick to it; many are also critical of the labels that appear with such sexual polarity. Renaud says he doesn't think "people should have to choose sexualities or labels. For me, it is a matter of choosing an individual I'm attracted to."

Szkambara says she's always viewed people simply as sexual — "how they express it doesn't matter. If sexuality is a display of love, affection, desire and caring," she says, "then I don't think I should be forced to direct these emotions only toward one sex."

Carole Desjardins (not her real name) is a third year Arts student at McGill who says she "doesn't bother" to define her sexuality, although she is attracted to members of both sexes. "Labels are really stifling; I'm not pigeon-holeable and I don't like feeling that I have to be. I'm attracted to people as people, not for their genitals. But there are emotional and political factors which cause me to relate better to women, so most of my relationships have been with women," she says.

Byrnes says there are many times when labels have a positive function — "when they are used to recognize and validate the full truth of one's sexuality." Such usage means one is clearly making a choice one is proud of, despite the possible isolation and discrimination one may experience as a result. "Our culture is so afraid and suppressive around the issue of bisexuality. There is more of a range of sexualities than our culture is willing to recognize — that's why it's important for bisexuals to label themselves as such. It's a way of being visible and a way to validate one's own uniqueness," says Byrnes.

But, Byrnes adds, labeling also has potential pitfalls. "When I feel I have to sleep with a woman soon, or I'm no longer or not really bisexual; when the label becomes a prison you can't deviate from — then it's a pitfall."

"There is this idea," says Siepniewicz, "that you're not a real bisexual unless you sleep with both sexes equally." Few bisexuals define themselves as such because "pure" 50/50 bisexuality is extremely unlikely in a society that emphasizes monogamous relationships, she says.

"But there are so many ways in which bisexuality manifests itself. You can be attracted to both sexes," says Siepniewicz, "but that doesn't mean you have to be involved with members of both sexes all the time. You can be celibate and bisexual; you can be in the middle of a long-term monogamous relationship with a member of the opposite sex and still fantasize about members of the same sex."

Although there is an obvious need for a supportive community for bisexual men and women, Siepniewicz is quick to point out that "bisexuals are so different from each other that a homogeneous sort of bisexual community could never exist."

But to account for and celebrate their diversity, as well as deal with their specific concerns, bisexuals agree that both bisexual women and men should start up their own support groups, separately or within the lesbian, gay, and women's movements in order to raise awareness about issues related to bisexuality.

"There is a need for more honest dialogue between all sides of this issue," says Maggie de Vries. "Misunderstanding, resentment, and a lack of trust between bisexual and gay communities will continue until bisexuals, homosexuals, and heterosexuals start openly discussing and dealing with their concerns regarding bisexuality." And, adds Mary Louise Adams, "as long as bisexuals are invisible, their concerns will be ignored by straights and lesbians and gay men."

Bisexual women and men have a busy agenda. Stereotypes must be combated, bisexual visibility must be increased, and a legitimate place in society for bisexuals must be created. Meanwhile, more and more bisexuals are starting to come out of the woodwork and speak up about their specific concerns. As gay activist Thomas Burnside reflects, "maybe this symbolizes a new phase of the movement, a new stage of liberation."

Bisexuals hope he's right.

To Remake the World: On Coalitions
By Beth Reba Weise

Originally from the second North American (now National) Bisexual Network mailing. Reprinted in Bisexuality: News, Views, and Networking, *August 19, 1988. Used with permission.*

One would expect it to be easy. A small number of people, under a hundred, all from North America and all native speakers of the same language, decide to form a group. The basis of their coming together is the fact that loving and being sexual with both women and men is a possibility in their lives. Not that love and sex seem such difficult things, needful of a group to champion them. But they are, and we must. The right to love is not easily given in our world.

So we come together, spanning climate zones and mindsets, for the pleasure of one another's company, to find people for whom *whom* we love is less important than the fact *that* we love.

But this coming together is not an easy thing, as simple as the concept seems on the surface. We share feelings for women and men in common, but little else. We are a wildly diverse collection of people. Our numbers include staunch lesbians and gay activists, comfortable in their bisexuality, as well as people for whom the notion of telling just a friend is overwhelming, much less telling the world. We include adamant advocates of nonmonogamy, and those who are happily partnered.

We are radical feminists who haven't done political work with men in years, and those who find it unconscionable to work in sex-segregated groups. People working fervently for the revolution to come, some who don't expect ever to see it and those working just as hard to see that it never gets here. We are Communists, Socialists, Anarchists, Democrats, Republicans, Libertarians and probably some who want to see the monarchy re-established.

Our group contains women and men for whom feminism is the base-line for discussion and those who don't know what the word means. People who think everyone should always have two lovers

---

of either sex and those with no lovers at all. People with AIDS and people with homophobia — both deadly diseases. And sadly, we are also overwhelmingly white, and while this makes some of us secretly more comfortable, it makes others of us redouble our efforts to include representatives of that quarter of the population of Canada and the United States who aren't.

A black lesbian feminist once defined coalition building as working with people who might otherwise want to kill you. There's truth in what she said. It can be bloody, painful work. It means paring away everything nonessential, cutting down to the bone of what you believe in — and then trying to bridge the gap between that and someone else's most deeply held beliefs. All in the name of coalition, the notion that we are stronger together than we are apart.

It is difficult, distressing, and deeply important work. Without being able to work together and forge bonds of understanding among ourselves, how can we ask that the larger society understand and accept us?

Working in coalition means staring the devil in the face. It means letting go of small fears, learning to trust and compromise. And it means being extremely clear about what cannot be compromised. Above all it means a commitment to the greater ideal of unity, and a willingness to stay in the fray to achieve it.

In forming the North American Bisexual Network, we are building a coalition. We're entering into a process that may take years. We will be changed and transformed by it. At times we will certainly want to strangle each other. But by our work we will be remaking the world.

June, 1988
San Francisco

The Borderline Bisexual Blues

By Amanda Udis-Kessler
Transcribed by T. Geller

Swing - Not Straight!

Verse 1

Let me sing you a sto - ry of the peo- ple that I love—— And the pre -jud-iced ex- clu - sion that I face. I'm not wel come in ei-ther the straight world or the gay No com mun - i - ty has gi - ven me a place. Well, some times I love wo-men and some times I love men And the pas - sion is - n't some - thing I con trol Oh folks have told me why—— it's such a pro blem to be bi But I need both sides to know that I'm whole.

Chorus

C   E7

I'm not real-ly straight and I'm not real-ly gay———— All

Am   D

I am is me and what more can I say?———————— You

C/G   E7

tell me "Make your mind up!" but how can I choose?——— I

F   Fm   4th x to Coda

can't play it straight or gay, each way I lose.——— I got the

G   G7   1., 2. C   3. C

Bor - der - line Bi - sex - u - al Blues.   When it

Bridge

Am   D   D/F♯

comes to gay rights po - li - tics, I put in my time: No

Gm   C   C/E

mat - ter what you call me, my sex life is a crime. I

Fm   B♭7

or - ga- nize for mar- ches, put the fly- ers on the wall But their

E♭   D   D.C. al Coda

ti- tles don't in- clude the word "Bi sex - u-al" at all. Oh I

37

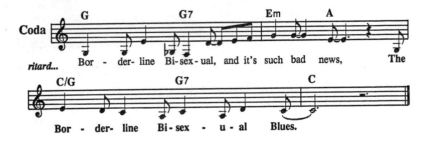

Coda

ritard... Bor - der-line Bi-sex-ual, and it's such bad news, The

Bor - der-line Bi-sex-u-al Blues.

Verse 2

You think I could identify with straights half the time
Well that's not as easy as it sounds
To them I'm just a deviant — no matter how much
Or else I'm just playing around (and really normal).
Well when I get involved they might be supportive —
If the person's of the opposite sex
And don't we know that these days when it comes to AIDS
Bisexuals are really the threat.

Chorus

Verse 3

To gays I'm just experimenting, not one of them,
Or else they say I'm "not quite out."
They say that I can always pass for straight if I need to,
So how can I know what oppression's about?
If I'm seeing a woman, I could just say I'm a lesbian*
But that kind of deceiving really hurts
But if I'm open with my lover, and she thinks I'll go straight
She'll make sure she gets to say goodbye first.

Chorus

Bridge

* If sung by a man: "If I'm seeing a man, I could just say that I'm gay."

When it comes to gay rights politics, I put in my time
No matter what you call me, my sex life is a crime
I organize for marches, put the flyers on the wall
But their titles don't include the word "Bisexual" at all.

Verse 4
Oh I can't deny my feelings and I don't want to lie
You know closets are intended for clothes.
There's not a fence I'm sitting on, I'm not "undecided,"
I'm bi and that's the way that it goes.
If you want to be fair, just respect me as a person
'Cause when the whole mess is over and done
There will be a day when the labels don't matter
And we'll relax and have a whole lot of fun.

Chorus

Coda

Anyone interested in purchasing tapes of this song or performing it should contact the composer-copyright holder, Amanda Udis-Kessler, in care of Times Change Press, P.O. Box 1380, Ojai, CA 93023.

Where The Boys Aren't:
The Shortage of Men in the Bi Movement
An interview with Robyn Ochs
by Gary North (used with permission of Ms. Ochs and Mr. North)

This article was originally published in the July 27, 1988 issue of Bisexuality: News, Views, and Networking. *In this part, Ms. Ochs talks about the differences between the two major genders in regards to bi/gay politics as well as some of her own experiences with the Boston Bisexual Women's and the East Coast Bisexual networks. Another part of the interview begins on page 9.*

Q: Have you drawn any conclusions or given any thought to bisexuality as a "movement" especially as it regards leadership — men vs. women? The reason I ask this is that in my research, I kept running into *women* who were taking leadership roles or leading the movement — or *a* bi movement — and men were few and far between. Do you have some thoughts about that, or are my perceptions wrong?

A: Your perceptions are very right. I think that the trend you see in the bisexual community is the same trend you see in the gay/lesbian community: that lesbians tend to be feminists, and gay men tend not to be . . . they tend not to be activists, they tend not to be feminists.

Also, I think men are in a position of relative power — they earn more money, they have more access to things than women do — and if you're a woman and you become a lesbian or become bisexual, I think it's almost impossible to do that without tying it in with the larger politics of society. . . . For a woman to be a lesbian or be bisexual involves challenging a lot of society's assumptions.

If you look at the gay male community, it's much better funded, it's much more based on being consumers. There are a lot of bars, of clothing stores, a lot of stuff that caters to gay men. If you go to Provincetown, you see that there are 40 men's bars and one women's bar. And for whatever reason, the gay male culture has — or was, because I think it's changing now with AIDS — but it was . . . a "party" culture. It was a culture of going out and seeing lots of different people, spending money, and going dancing, going to Provincetown, to the baths, whatever.

And if you look at the women's culture, it's tied in very closely with feminism. If you look at what lesbians do for fun, they work in battered women's shelters. Men go to the bars, and women go to shelters. Women — lesbians and bisexuals — are involved with women's centers. I see so much more a kind of non-profit orientation in the women's community. And I think that it feeds upon itself. If you come out as a gay or bisexual man, and you go out to meet people, the culture is there now. And to fit into the existing culture, you kind of change yourself to be that way. And if you go out to the women's community, the same thing happens, although I don't know if it's something that has to be. It's kind of the way things have developed and so they are.

I think things are changing because of AIDS, and men are becoming more political because of AIDS. I think you've seen the gay community finally pull together. I think you see a hell of a lot more gay men working for the AIDS Action Committee and other kinds of groups than you would have six years ago. . . . I think AIDS, in a way, has really politicized the gay male community in a way that it hasn't been before.

And there are tons of exceptions: look at the whole fairy movement — men who reject traditional male roles and who are very feminist — and the changing-men's organizations. There have always been feminist men and there have always been women who do nothing but go to the bars. But the communities as a whole are so different from each other.

Q: How closely do you work with the Boston Bisexual Men's Network? How involved are the men in the East Coast Bisexual Network? Or more generally, how much contact do you have with bisexual men politically and socially?

A: The men in the bisexual movement who I know — the ones I choose to know — are a rather small key group of organizers, and those are the men who are feminists and those are the men who are political, and those are the men who are activists. They will say, and I would agree, that the vast majority of men who come through the BBMN are completely apolitical — most of them are closeted — so the men I choose to associate with are the core group of activists, because I like what they're doing. They themselves are discouraged by the lack of feminist consciousness, of activist consciousness of the men who come in.

Q: Is it at all divisive that there are two groups, male and female, rather than just one Boston bisexual group?

A: I think that while there would be some advantages of having one group, the advantages of having two outweigh those of having one.

Q: One of the things that struck me when I was first doing the research for this article was a slight fear that not only was the movement — if there is a movement — becoming dichotomized but that it would be a bisexual *women's* movement, as compared to a bisexual movement in general. What are your feelings about that?

A: Well, I think there are, have been, and will continue to be bisexual men in the larger movement. Unfortunately, I think that their numbers are going to remain small in comparison.

Q: Because of the politicization that women feel regarding the feminist aspects of it?

A: That's one part of it. Another part of it is that in this day and age, it's very scary to be a gay or bi man.

Q: Why is it more scary than to be a bi woman?

A: Because bi men are perceived as being carriers of AIDS to the heterosexual community. They're being scapegoated right now. Both gay and bisexual men are being scapegoated as being the ones who are somehow responsible for spreading AIDS. So if you're a bisexual man and you're going to get involved in a relationship with a woman, and if you're honest and open about who you are, there's a good chance that women won't get involved with you. And at the very least you'd have a whole lot of processing to do about it, whereas if you're a bisexual woman, bisexual women are not a high-risk group.

Q: How do you feel society currently perceives bisexual women?

A: I think that one of the reasons lesbians are frightening to hetero-sexual men is because they have said, "We don't need you, and we're not going to define ourselves by you or around you." I don't think they're quite as afraid of bisexual women.

Q: What about other women in the feminist movement: not necessarily the lesbian movement , but the general movement?

A: I think that bisexuality is scary to people because it challenges our simple categories. I think it makes people question themselves. If you're told there are only two letters in the alphabet, A and B, and you know that you've got A in you, it's one thing, but when you find out there's A-, B+, it opens up questions most people don't really deal with. So I think that's true of straight women not only in the feminist community but that it's pretty true across the board. That's one of the reasons that bisexuality is so frightening to people, because it makes things so complicated.

Q: Did you at any point ever think of trying to define yourself as lesbian to be accepted by a lesbian community or to make your life simpler?

A: I never did. I identify as a lesbian, but I identify as a bisexual lesbian.

Q: A number of women have used that term. How do you define it?

A: I think that being a lesbian is a lot more than who you sleep with. It implies a whole cultural component of "where do you put your priorities," what are your politics, what kind of concerts do you like to go to?

Q: As compared with being a bisexual feminist? I wonder if women who say they are bisexual lesbians mean they are bisexual feminists, and they're using the wrong word. Does one who is a bisexual necessarily have to become politicized and be a feminist, especially if one is a woman?

A: Not if you don't think too hard about it. And again, there are degrees of being a feminist and there are degrees of politicization. For example, I have a hard time understanding why someone would want to be part of a political party that doesn't want them to have rights. "Gay Republican" for example — I see a contradiction there.

It's interesting that when you call yourself a bisexual lesbian,

43

you get two sets of reactions. You get people who say, "Oh, that's good, I'm glad you're calling yourself that." And then you get people who say, "How dare you . . . ." So it's not necessarily a popular label to choose.

. . . [BBWN] did a survey in 1984, and we asked people about their politics — we asked them whether they considered themselves feminists, and 95 percent of them said yes. I think activism and feminism go hand in hand, most of the time. But then again,

. . . there are people like Phyllis Schlafley who are activists who are not feminists.

Q: Do you anticipate being with BBWN and ECBN and all those other acronyms for the long term?

A: I think that activism has to be seen in the long term. I think that anything you work toward is going to take a long time, and this is something I'll have to work on the rest of my life. I think I'll be changing my focus over time. I've already changed my focus. Last year, when I started graduate school, I had to draw some limits, because I work full-time and I was going to graduate school half-time and doing some other political work, so where was BBWN going to fit? So last year, I did a lot, but a lot less than I used to — I coordinated the volunteer nights and I did speaking engagements and workshops and I went to the coordinating committee. And I coordinated the fundraiser. I used to run all the introductory meetings, too. But I no longer maintain the mailing list; I no longer go to every single activity. So I have drawn some limits. I give two nights a month now on the average throughout the year.

Q: Are there enough people in BBWN that you feel secure about its future?

A: It's something that comes in waves.

Q: I always think of the Bi Center in San Francisco that existed and then seemed to disappear.

A: In BBWN's history, we've had a couple of points where the energy was very low and where no new people came in, and we've had times of surges of energy, too. We've probably had two lulls and three surges. So during the lulls I get scared.

I believe very strongly that if everybody does a little, then nobody will have to do a lot. That's part of a good organization. And that's the goal that every organization should strive to achieve — to figure out ways to divide the work in such a way that nobody is overwhelmed. We've been increasingly successful in doing that. But we still have a long way to go, and I think that it's a constant process. I firmly belive that everybody should be stuffing envelopes, that nobody's to the point that they don't have to stuff envelopes, because envelopes are important. So I think I'll always be stuffing envelopes for the network, but I would also like not to do it every month. So when you ask what my goal is and where I'd like to go with the network, I'd like the opportunity to do what I'm doing, but I'd like to see the network develop in such a way that more and more people take responsibility.

Another thing that I wanted to say is that I believe very strongly that to be aware of your minority status in any area makes you aware of the connections between your discrimination and other people's. In other words, to be discriminated against as a bisexual should make you draw the connections between homophobia and biphobia and racism and sexism because they're all connected in that they're all categorical judgments on a group of people, and once you're in a group that's categorically judged, you know that it's wrong. I mean, I know that it's wrong to say that all bisexuals are promiscuous or all bisexuals are confused or all bisexuals are anything. Once you're aware, once you're the victim of that kind of categorization, I find it hard not to become aware of the fact that other kinds of discrimination are categorical and false — racism, sexism, ageism, or ableism.

For example, if you're a person of color, if you saw those connections, you'd have to stop being homophobic, you'd have to stop being sexist, once you start thinking in those terms, because they're all so connected. And we're not going to get rid of just one of those things. You have to get rid of homophobia and racism and sexism and heterosexism and whatever because they're all so connected, and they're all false.

In BBWN, for example, I think there's the realization that that's true.

Q: And where do you go from there?

A: You go to BiCEP [the Bi Committee Engaging in Politics]. I think BBWN needs to stay the way it is because I think we need to have an organization that appeals to all women and that is a safe space for all women regardless of their politics or where they are in their own thinking. But I think BiCEP is the next step . . . I feel that BBWN is pretty secure. I mean, we may go through times where we have to curtail one activity or another or where we decide to change our focus, but we've been around for five years, and that's a long time. And there are more groups around the country than there have ever been. So we're doing great. But changing the world takes a long time.

Q: Well, you've made a good start.

A: I think we have.

The Bisexual Potential
by Bill Himelhoch

This is an excerpt from the introduction to Mr. Himelhoch's unpublished manuscript of bisexual interviews entitled The Bisexual Potential. *It is very similar to a segment of the radio program* "The Bisexual Voice in Literature," *which he produced for broadcast in 1988 for WBAI, the Pacifica radio station in New York City. Used with permission.*

A bisexual potential exists in the human race.

It does not awaken in the life of every individual, of course. Many people feel a compelling sexual attraction only for one sex, be it the opposite or the same sex. In other persons the bisexual potential may stir only fleetingly, a brief ripple dancing across the surface of their sexuality without consequences or need for further thought.

For the rest of humanity, the bisexual potential is vigorous enough to require some kind of response. For people who are leading conventional lives, their judgments and tolerances being shaped by the traditions of the dominant society, the presence of bisexual feelings is disruptive. Their homosexual feelings are condemned by religions, governments, and other social structures, leading them to suppress their same-sex feelings.

The cost of squelching a part of sexuality varies greatly. It would appear that for most people, the price to be paid for shunting aside their homosexual feelings is no greater than the price all of us are accustomed to paying for blocking desires and impulses outlawed by the cultural norms we live by. Many others, unfortunately, are caught in a prolonged and morbid struggle against the uncontrollable outcropping of unwanted feelings.

The pressure to be attracted exclusively to one sex is exerted not only on overt heterosexuals. Men and women who live in gay subcultures are apt to comply to a similar prohibition. Attractions to the opposite sex are presumed to be subversive to the solidarity that is transforming a marginal group of outcasts into a vigorous community with growing political and economic stature. Vital social ties to this community may be jeopardized by alliances to the heterosexual world and its hateful prejudices.

The massive denial of the bisexual potential has prevailed against human feelings since the Christianization of the Roman Empire. Before this mood took hold in European history, an individual's sexual attraction to women and men was not a subject for comment. The bisexual potential existed as unobtrusively as the oxygen we breathe. There was nothing that had to be done about it except, as in every society, to prevent abusive behavior. Among the celebrated achievements of Athens was its ethical ideal for balancing matrimony and same-sex friendships. Eroticism between males and conjugal relations between husbands and wives were governed by a single standard of right conduct.

The liberation movements of the past several decades have gone far to correct the condemnation of human feelings. For younger persons especially, tolerance of all sexual feelings is considered to be necessary for achieving self-integration and wholeness. They are bravely staking out their claim for a sexuality free of fear, self-condemnation, and shame.

Academia
Looks at
<u>Bisexuality</u>

Tidbits!

"We shall not really succeed in discarding the straitjacket of our own cultural beliefs about sexual choice if we fail to come to terms with the well-documented, normal human capacity to love members of both sexes."
    Margaret Mead.

"Homosexuality was invented by a straight world dealing with its own bisexuality."
    Kate Millet (in Bisexual Lives*).*

". . . Until the privilege of heterosexuality is ended, 'bisexual' is not the neutral term it is implied to be."
    Tom Kennedy, from "Homophobia in the Left," Originally printed in the New American Movement Newspaper, *Summer 1975, reprinted in* For Men Against Sexism: A Book of Readings.

Like homosexuality, bisexuality can be poison to the heterosexist power structure. Bisexuality makes everyone more difficult to control, to coerce. Bisexuality confounds the paradigm that pits straights and the so-called "normal" people against the "deviants."
    Lucy, from Boston.

Bisexuality in an Essentialist World:
Toward an Understanding of Biphobia
by Amanda Udis-Kessler

This paper was presented by the author at Yale University on April 14, 1989. Used with permission. © 1989 by the author.

Imagine this. You are at work on a lesbian/gay political or educational event. Or, possibly, you are involved in AIDS education or activism. You work as hard as anyone else, and you are as committed as anyone else. However, your sexuality is denied, if not actually disparaged. You are considered an oppressor and sometimes a spy; your concerns are thought to be different and threatening. Some of the people with whom you interact think you shouldn't be part of lesbian/gay/AIDS work at all. In their minds, you are one of the "fence-sitters, traitors, cop-outs, closet cases, people whose primary goal in life is to retain 'heterosexual privilege,' power-hungry cold-hearted seducers who use and discard their same-sex lovers like so many Kleenex." [1] If nothing else, you are responsible for the spread of AIDS. Imagine. All of this, simply because you identify as bisexual. [2]

There are two reasons why lesbian/gay communities would do well to examine, and ultimately unlearn, their biphobia. First, gaybashings and gay-related murders are increasing around the

[1] Orlando, Lisa. "Loving Whom We Choose: Bisexuality." *Gay Community News*, January 25, 1984: 8.

[2] Of course, there are people whose bisexuality does seem to represent a stage on the way to exclusive homosexuality or who are "experimenting." And there are bisexual people who deeply hurt their same sex lovers and whose lives appear to be about retaining heterosexual privilege. And there are gay men who abuse children and lesbians who want to be men. There is always a small minority which fits some of the stereotypes, but that minority clearly does not justify the existence of homophobia. The same is true of biphobia.

nation. The incidence of homophobia on college campuses has risen alarmingly. Sex and AIDS educators who insist on being honest about homosexuality have lost federal funding, and judges and officials around the country have made it clear that their bigotry will affect their judicial and legal decision-making. Gay religious groups are kicked out of churches; their clergy are sometimes forced to leave their orders, or are silenced. The Supreme Court has upheld sodomy laws and many states have refused to pass antidiscrimination laws for their lesbian, gay, and bisexual citizens. Twenty years after Stonewall, ten years after the assassination of Harvey Milk, there is a daunting amount of work to do, and lesbians and gays cannot afford to exclude anyone who wants to participate. This especially includes bisexuals, who share the same issues, and not just "half the time." We don't get half-gaybashed when we walk down the street with our same-sex lovers; we don't even get bashed half as often. We don't get half-fired from our jobs, or lose only half of our children in court battles. When HIV-positive, we don't progress to ARC and then stop, rather than getting full-blown AIDS. Lesbian/gay issues are our issues, and we want to work on them with lesbians and gay men. We can offer our strength, energy, and creativity. It's too dangerous a time to let biphobia get in the way of resources.

I said there were two reasons for unlearning biphobia. In the past few years, lesbian/gay communities have begun serious work on the racism and sexism which exists within every part of our culture. They have begun to acknowledge their power to oppress, as well as their experience of being oppressed. With the growth of coalitioning, they have taken up others' causes as others have taken up lesbian and gay causes. In this process, lesbians and gays are learning new ways to communicate and relate, ways that are not hierarchical and dualistic but that point forward to an egalitarian society. Looked at in this light, biphobia is just one more wall that needs to come down. Various arguments have been advanced as to why lesbians and gay men, no strangers to bigotry and persecution, should continue to malign anyone's sexuality. The claims are similar to some of those offered for homophobia: jealousy, fear of differences that one doesn't understand, fear that one might actually be bisexual. Today, I want to consider a possible explanation which goes beyond these and draws on sexual identity theory, specifically the essentialist/constructionist debate.[3]

This debate appears in various disciplines, and concerns the nature of someone's identity; for our purposes, the debate concerns the nature of sexuality. Essentialists will describe sexuality as an essence, or ontological category, while constructionists (properly called social constructionists) will claim that sexuality does not exist as a category in and of its own right, only as a facet of specific human lives and experiences. To the extent that sexuality is a category for the constructionist, it is a socially constructed one.

Plato's World of Forms is a metaphysical example of essentialism. To Plato, essence preceded existence. Goodness (or "The Good") transcended good acts, and, we may speculate, sandalness transcended any specific sandal. Goodness and sandalness were categories, forms from which discrete items and processes derived. A particular good act participated in goodness, and a particular sandal participated in sandalness. The good act and sandal in themselves were less significant than the forms from which they came.

Because we no longer work from the concept of a world of forms, modern essentialist language is somewhat different. Essence still precedes existence, but it is now described in biological, rather than metaphysical, terms. Essentialists describe sexual orientation as innate: a basic, individually immanent part of one's sex drive. That is, there is a predetermined orientational "core of truth" in any person, regardless of his or her sexual behavior. Note the normative dimensions of this outlook: it is as unnatural and perverted for a homosexual to engage in heterosexual sex as it is for a heterosexual to engage in homosexual sex. To an essentialist, sexual orientation is deterministic. The very phrase "sexual orientation" is essentialist in nature.

[3] I am indebted to Bill Marsiglio, currently of the University of Florida, Gainesville, Sociology Department, for introducing me to this debate as it affects sexuality.

Constructionism, in contrast, begins with empiricism: existence precedes essence. Sexual orientation, far from being a predetermined ontological category, is seen as a constructed descriptor of discrete acts. While the essentialist moved from the category to the specific example, the constructionist moves from the specific example to the category. In studying individuals and the societies in which they live, the constructionist encounters sexual scripts that vary with era and location. Moreover, even within a specific era and location, there can be variations on the sexual script. One's sexuality emerges throughout one's life in response to changing scripts and situations; it is relational. As Cliff Arnesen recently noted, "The process of socialization and sexual orientation are interwoven. They produce the many ways that men and women learn how and whom to love. In short, there is no universal 'map' on loving."[4] To a constructionist, sexual orientation is not deterministic; it is not simply the unfolding of a natural process. Rather, it is learned, contingent, unpredictable; the potential for change remains throughout every life. To a constructionist, sexuality is as sexuality does.

Consider the history of the sexual language we now use. The term "sexuality" did not appear in the Oxford English Dictionary until 1800. Although there has been homosexual behavior since animals became sexual, and certainly since people became sexual, the word "homosexuality" did not exist until 1869, and did not reach common usage until the 1890s. We talk now of "the love that dared not speak its name," but we would do well to remember that it had no name until about a century ago. The essentialist would argue that we discovered the category of homosexuality, much the same way scientists discovered oxygen and the heliocentric design of our solar system. The constructionist would argue that we constructed the category because it became useful to have such a category. Further, the constructionist would argue that there is no hard and fast distinction between heterosexuality and homosexuality.

Before I move into the history of this debate within lesbian/gay liberation, perhaps I should make my own bias on the debate clear.

[4] In a letter to *Gay Community News*, March 26 - April 1, 1989, p. 5.

I believe that sexuality is overdetermined and has both essentialist and constructionist roots. Nonetheless, I am primarily a constructionist. If we look at individuals across the span of their lives, we see the limitations of essentialism. At any given point in time, a person may experience what feels like an essential pull in a given direction, yet several years or decades later experience the exact reverse. The essentialist has no way to describe a woman who is happily heterosexual until age forty and happily homosexual thereafter, except to say that the first forty years didn't count in some way, did not represent the woman's true self. This seems unreasonable as well as demeaning; it delegitimates forty years of sexual experience which may have been very meaningful. Essentialism has been of even less help in understanding sexuality in non-Western cultures.

Constructionism seems to me the better way of describing human sexual capacity and variety, as long as its limitations are also clarified. Most specifically, while constructionism does imply fluidity across time and place, it does not *necessarily* imply willful choice or intentionality, either in an individual's life or in a given society. Cultures are not as malleable as we might like to think, and individuals who undergo sexual changes in their lives may have no sense of having chosen them. The issue of choice is extremely important, given that the constructionist suggestion of its possibility is the grounds upon which many essentialists criticize constructionism. Both essentialism and constructionism also have political limitations, which we will consider later; for now let us consider the part which the sexual-identity debate played in the history of our communities and political struggles.

Before Stonewall, lesbian and gay groups such as the Mattachine Society and Daughters of Bilitis attempted to show heterosexual society how similar heterosexuals and homosexuals were, as a way of gaining acceptance in society at large. The idea of proudly and openly creating a counterculture, or indeed, of taking radical political stances, was not common in the decades before Stonewall. The changing politics following Stonewall involved a drastic identity shift: lesbians and gay men went from assimilationism to an "ethnic" model of oppression and counterculture.

In this ethnic model, lesbians and gay men came to see themselves as a specific oppressed minority, much like any racial or ethnic minority in a white, racist society. They drew on the civil rights movement and its language to describe their situation and their newfound resistance; George Weinberg's coinage of the term "homophobia" strengthened the parallel with racism. In coming to understand themselves as an ethnic minority, lesbians and gay men began to stress the difference between themselves and heterosexual people, and to ground that difference in biology.[5] In fact, the constructionist view of sexuality, with its fluidity and its connotation of choice, threatened lesbians and gay men as soon as it was proposed. Constructionism challenged the "oppressed ethnic minority" approach by arguing that sexuality could not be compared to skin color as a natural phenomenon. To many lesbians and gay men, constructionism took away their greatest asset, the ethnic self-conception, and did not offer a sound replacement. It could too easily be utilized by homophobic leaders as an argument that lesbians and gay men could change and should therefore be forced to do so.

Constructionists replied that this view distorted the role that choice and intentionality may play in constructionism, in which the personal sexuality changes addressed need be neither chosen nor intentional — and certainly not forced by outside pressure or self-hatred. They further explained that they were not proposing the idea of "sexual preference," as though object choice were equivalent to choice of breakfast cereal; in a society of compulsory heterosexuality, a phrase that connoted choosing between equally accepted sexual options was inadequate and inaccurate. Communities replied that since their homophobic opponents would happily twist constructionism to discredit them, they needed an essentialist identity to strengthen themselves. Accuracy in sexual-identity description simply was not as important as the politics of the community. While sexual theorists continued the essentialist/constructionist

[5] Here I am indebted to Paul Horowitz's article, "Beyond the Gay Nation: Where Are We Marching?" *Out/Look*, Vol. 1, No. 1, Spring 1988, pp. 7-21.

debate in academic journals and other settings, community members lived essentialist lives, creating separatist culture and politics, putting their primary energy into the community and their primary trust in other lesbians and gay men.[6] Steven Epstein, as late as 1987, noted that "while constructionist theories have been preaching the gospel that the hetero/homosexual distinction is a social fiction, gays and lesbians, in everyday life and in political action, have been busy hardening the categories."[7] In 1989, AIDS activists, gay male culturalists, and lesbian separatists demonstrate the continuation of essentialism. While constructionism may represent the better description of human sexuality, the very elements which make lesbian/gay communities strong today — perhaps which make them possible as communities at all — are essentialist.

This history has been told many times; these connections have been made before by theorists on both sides of the debate. My claim is that this history can be linked with biphobia in lesbian/gay communities. We will need to take a somewhat roundabout path to see how this can be, beginning with the relationship between biphobia and the fear of being bisexual.

Consider a lesbian who has gone through a hard coming-out process, who has taken a long time to arrive at a sense of her identity and to settle into her local community. Or consider a gay man who can look back on a history of pain and homophobia, who was beaten up throughout high school, frozen out by parents, thrown out by landlords. Each of these people may have a hard time with bisexuality, especially if it is the bisexuality within themselves. The lesbian, finally secure in a lesbian identity, may not want to remain in touch with her bisexuality; it may threaten her sense of self and

---

[6] For the purposes of this paper, I have chosen to ignore the male-female splits in the early post-Stonewall period: divisions of thought, action, and community which were very important in many ways but which did not have an appreciable impact on this question.

[7] Epstein, Steven. "Gay Politics, Ethnic Identity: The Limits of Social Constructionism." *Socialist Review* 93/4 (May-August 1987): 12.

her community location. Likewise, the gay man with the scars of homophobia may be horrified to discover his bisexuality. What, then, was this pain about? Do the experiences that shaped him mean nothing? Was there an easier way? And should he have taken it? Both of these people have gone through pain and soul-searching to reach their identities, which provide them with a sense of unity, a social location, and a political commitment; to see those identities fluctuate would be unnerving, and would threaten the meaning of their personal histories.

Likewise, lesbian/gay communities have gone through tremendous growing pains, indeed, are built on a great deal of shared pain. The communities and their struggles only make sense if the pain was in some way the inevitable product of being oneself in a homophobic and heterosexist society. Note that the essentialist view of sexuality seems to be required in this equation. Just as bisexuality would threaten the two people described above, the fluidity and connotation of choice within constructionism would seem to challenge both the history and the future of a community built on pain.

Now we can begin to see the threat posed by bisexuality somewhat more clearly. The charge that bisexuals retain "heterosexual privilege" does not need to come from a closet bisexual. The idea that bisexuality destroys the point of gay rights is not a product of fear of the unknown. Rather, the biphobia reflected in these statements arises from the fear of constructionism. Community-oriented individuals, protective of the essentialist view of sexuality that seems to give rhyme and reason to their communities, equate the fluidity and apparent choice-making of bisexuality with that of constructionism, and see only a threat to that which they hold dear. Bisexuality, then, signifies constructionism, and the assumed link between the two is not, in reality, entirely absent. Constructionism does posit that everyone has, if not the experience of living a bisexual life, than at least the potential to do so. Moreover, constructionism makes the claim that one's sexuality is not necessarily firmly set at age five, or even at age fifty. While it is basic to constructionism that no mode of sexuality or object choice is better than another, bisexuality occupies a place of importance in construction-ism that it does not in essentialism.

If bisexuality signifies constructionism and constructionism is seen as a threat to some lesbians and gay men, bisexuals will be scapegoated sooner or later. In the presence of a walking example of constructionism, angers and fears quite unrelated to the individual have a chance to surface. Lesbians and gay men are as capable of prejudice as any heterosexual bigot. Moreover, because the bisexual threat involves fluidity, the response to it can be to stereotype in a particularly problematic way. To understand some of the misconceptions about bisexuals and bisexuality, we need to return to the social sciences and consider the idea of reification.

Reification, a constructionist concept, describes the hardening of a social construct into an ontological category in the worldview of a set of people.[8] As a socially constructed behavior or idea is institutionalized, society comes to forget its original social construction and perceives it as natural and without a beginning in time. That which is historically contingent comes to be seen as inevitable. A government gains power and rewrites history around itself. A religious practice which arose because of a practical and culture-specific need is touted as a divine revelation for all people.

Reification is a way of explaining how people give social constructs ontological validity. I noted before that the terms "sexuality" and "homosexuality" are recent developments in human sexual history, and that constructionists would argue that we created them when we needed them. Moreover, they would argue that the creation of those terms played a part in the reification of sexual acts, and in the artificial division between homosexuality and heterosexuality to which I alluded before. Herein lies an explanation for some of the stereotypes about bisexuality. Consider that heterosexuality and homosexuality would be easy to reify compared to bisexuality. They seem to make sense as categories. But how does one reify fluidity? How does one make a category of the potential to have either kind of relationship? The essentialist answer is to

[8] I am indebted to Deb Reiner for this way of describing reification.

change bisexuality from a potential-for-either to a requirement-for-both identity, and this, in fact, is what happened. The lore which developed described bisexuals as people who could not be satisfied with either sex, but who had to be involved with both, usually at the same time. Bisexuals became stereotyped as swingers who eschewed commitment and were promiscuous because there was no other way to categorically describe the bisexual drive that paralleled the homosexual or heterosexual drive. We have already seen how essentialists had put up a fence between homosexuality and heterosexuality. Then they froze the motion which bisexuals made from one side to the other, and began calling us fence-sitters!

I've tried to present here a way of understanding biphobia among lesbians and gay men which is linked to questions of sexual identity and political community. I want to take time now to consider where some of these questions of identity and community might go from here. First, I want to look at certain political problems which essentialism and constructionism pose.

In order for constructionism to reclaim some authority in lesbian/gay communities, it will have to prove that it is gay-positive and, more importantly, gay culture-positive. Its value-free position as a purely descriptive social science tool is not likely to be of help to these communities today. Essentialism, for all of its limitations, has allowed them to provide support and encouragement for gay children without wondering whether they will be gay throughout their lives. Moreover, as I said before, many of the elements which make the communities what they are would be considered essentialist. If constructionism is to be taken seriously, it must strengthen the communities as well as helping people to grow beyond them.

Essentialism, which has pointed out how well constructionism can be twisted to justify denying lesbians and gay men their rights, can also be twisted by bigots, and in a more dangerous way. Attempts to justify racism[9], slavery and sexism have historically

[9] Neo-racism, which blames the victim by describing the awful ghetto conditions under which many people of color live, still avoids questions of institutional exploitation (why they live so badly), and thus is

been based on biological essentialism; only in the last decade or so have they touched on sociology or constructionism for their justification. Theories of biology-based sexual deviancy are the more dangerous for their apparent blandness, which effectively covers a great deal of homophobia. If a "gay gene," chromosome, nutritional deficiency or other biological difference were actually found, scientists would undoubtedly receive large grants from religious leaders and politicians to engineer it out or otherwise get rid of it. The fact that one has not been found and, by constructionist reckonings, will not be, is not the end of the problem. Essentialists have to face up to the danger of essentialism, as well as constructionism, in homophobic hands.

Eve Sedgwick has suggested that the essentialist/constructionist terminology is no longer useful, and that language such as minoritizing and universalizing would be more appropriate.[10] We would then ask not from whence sexuality comes, but rather to how many people is is the homo/heterosexual question important. To minoritize is to argue that a small number of people are affected by it, while to universalize is to affirm that questions of sexual identity are of import to a great number of people. To universalize means to go well beyond the ethnic minority identity and resultant separatism of American lesbian/gay communities; because of this it may be a useful approach for the future, both in terms of describing ourselves and defining our issues.

We lesbians and gay men and bisexuals are, after all, not an ethnic minority, and when we call ourselves one we forget that we include every existing ethnic and racial group on the planet, as well as every justice-seeking cause. We are black South Africans fighting apartheid, Asian-Americans fighting racism, and Latin Americans

─────

still racism. It is called "neo-racism" to distinguish it from the biological arguments for the inferiority of people of color which constituted traditional racism.

[10] Eve Sedgwick, "Some Axioms for a Gay Theory," address given at Emerson Hall, Harvard University, April 13, 1989.

fighting imperialism. We are Palestinians fighting for national rights and Jews the world over fighting antisemitism. These issues, then, are our issues, for they concern lesbian and gay and bisexual people. Of course, we are also white South Africans who support apartheid, racist Americans, imperialist North Americans and Europeans. We are also anti-Palestinian Zionists in Israel and anti-semites in every country. We can choose how universal our self-definition should be. In the same way, we are not the limited, if united, community that separatism would seem to indicate. Only a segment of gay and bisexual people are represented in lesbian/gay ghettos; many of the others are in ghettos of poverty, abuse, and despair. We are women fighting sexism and we are people who perpetuate sexism and benefit from it. We are poor people in a classist society and well-off people who like the current economic structure. If we are truly represented by the ratio of one in ten, then as of 1987, almost three and a half million people living below the poverty line were gay, four million hungry people were gay, and four hundred thousand homeless people were gay.[11] Economic justice issues such as unemployment wages, quality health care and housing for the homeless then also become part of our responsibility to our community. If we are truly to universalize, we may need to turn our attention to issues of race, class, and international stratification, for these are our issues in the broadest sense. We have drawn heavily on lesbian, gay, and bisexual figures from the past and from around the world to build up our culture, pride, and resources, whether we mean pre-Reformation or pre-Stonewall, whether we mean medieval Jewish poets, ancient Greek athletes, or Native American holy people. When we universalize, we offer some of our strength, creativity, and hope to the future, and to the rest of the world. It's only a fair exchange.

In closing, I want to say a few things about unlearning biphobia.

[11] From David Fair's address at the Seventh Annual Black Men & White Men Together Convention in Milwaukee, Wisconsin, in the summer of 1987; excerpts were run in a spring 1988 issue of *Gay Community News* under the title "We the People/We the 25 Million."

Homophobia education is extremely similar to biphobia education. All of us, bisexuals as well as lesbians and gay men, ask people to listen to our stories and trust that we are better equipped to describe ourselves and our lives than a bigot with an antigay or antibi agenda. Whatever the bigot's sexuality, he or she is no authority if his or her words are spoken out of hatred and fear. Our sexual differences from society at large do not imply differences in gender identity, culture, morality, or politics.[12] None of us chooses our sexual attractions, but each of us must choose how we respond to them; for any of us to hide our sexuality is tantamount to self-hatred. We ask people who hate or fear us to undergo a process of learning and acceptance. We hope that this process will be neither too difficult nor too time-consuming; the faster and more easily we overcome prejudice against alternative forms of sexuality, the more time and energy we will have to devote to other important issues and causes. Specifically, those of us who are bisexual do not want to take over lesbian/gay environments or use bisexual concerns to shut out lesbian/gay concerns, regardless of what some biphobes may say. We do not think the entire world is, or ought to be, bisexual; we only want the same respect that any lesbian or gay man would legitimately request. Or any other human being.

Today we may be justifiably proud of who we are and of how far we have come. Let us celebrate our sexualities in all of their rich variety. Let us think about what lies ahead, and remember that we who are lesbians and gay men and bisexual people have an important role to play in building our future. Finally, let us work together in peace; God knows the world needs the healing that we can bring.

[12] "Bisexuality does not exist as either a social institution or a psychological 'truth.' It exists only as a catch-all term for different erotic and social patterns whose common ground is an attempt to combine homo- and heterosexuality in a variety of ways. The term 'bisexual,' then, merely tells us that someone can or does eroticize both men and women. It does not tell us anything about the morality or politics of that person." Valverde, Marianna. *Sex, Power, and Pleasure.* Toronto: Women's Press, 1985: 119.

Sexual Orientation:
A Multivariable Dynamic Process
Fritz Klein, M.D.
Barry Sepekoff, Ph.D.
Timothy J. Wolf, Ph.D.

Drs. Klein and Wolf were the editors of The Journal of Homosexuality's *special issue on bisexuality (vol. 11, 1/2, 1985), from which this article was taken (with permission of the publisher).© 1985.*

Abstract. Theory and research concerning sexual orientation have been restricted in scope and influence by the lack of clear and widely accepted definitions of terms like heterosexual, bisexual, and homosexual. In an attempt to better demarcate and understand the complexities of human sexual attitudes, emotions, and behavior, the Klein Sexual Orientation Grid (KSOG) was developed and administered. The KSOG is composed of seven variables that are dimensions of sexual orientation, each of which is rated by the subject as applying to the present, past, or ideal. Analysis of the data from subjects who filled out the KSOG in *Forum* magazine indicated that the instrument was a reliable and valid research tool which took into consideration the multivariable and dynamic aspects of sexual orientation.

Theoretical positions regarding sexual orientation have been problematic because they have rigidly demarcated particular orientations, derived norms from clinical populations, and often been biased. Research instruments investigating sexual orientation tended to be as limited as the theoretical positions they were based on. Researchers have failed operationally or conceptually to define sexual orientation, by not providing clear or consistent definitions. This study gives evidence that sexual orientation cannot be reduced to a bipolar or even tripolar process, but must be recognized within a dynamic and multivariate framework.

Rigid dichotomization of sexual orientation has been the usual practice. Most theory and research have viewed people as either heterosexual or not. The idea that bisexuality was nonexistent was supported and perpetuated by Freud (1910), Bieber (1976), Krafft-Ebing ([1912] 1965) and Ellis (1965). Although Freud believed that all persons have bisexual capacities, he also believed that patients would cling to claims of bisexuality in order to avoid coming to terms with their homosexuality. As Freud (1910) stated: "A man's heterosexuality will not tolerate homosexuality" (p.472). According to the Freudian viewpoint, the ultimate sexual adjustment of the patient was either heterosexual or homosexual.

Heterosexual bias is closely related to the strict demarcation of sexual orientation. According to Freud ([1905] 1961), heterosexuality consisted of normal behavior and homosexuality of deviant behavior. Just as Freud viewed adult homosexuality as arrested development, Krafft-Ebing ([1912] 1965) viewed it as pathological and characterized congenital inversion as a "functional sign of degeneration" using degeneration in the evolutionary sense of falling away from the genus (pp. 187-188).

The view of homosexuality as deviance was based on data from the clinical populations. Freud based much of his theory on his observations of patients, primarily female, who sought psychotherapy. Bieber, studying the factors contributing to homosexuality, arrived at his conclusions as a result of his study of male patients in psychoanalysis. The first person to question the use of clinical samples was Hooker (1969). Based on her study of the environmental components of homosexuality, Hooker concluded that inferences drawn from psychiatric samples could not be applied to a nonclinical homosexual population.

As the flaws of theoretical perspectives based on clinical samples are revealed, a less rigid and biased view of sexual orientation comes into focus. Sound psychological and cross-cultural studies support the theoretical base of bisexuality. Anna Freud (1971) argued that the sex of an individual's masturbatory fantasies is the criterion for ascertaining sexual preference, adding that persons are capable of fantasizing about both sexes. This position is well documented in the findings of Kinsey (Kinsey, Pomeroy & Martin 1948). Mead (1975) referred to the normal capacity of persons to love members of both sexes. These perspectives are significant in light of empirical findings by Klein (1978) that there are between thirty and forty million persons in the United States who have sexual attraction to or behavior with both sexes.

A less rigid view of sexual orientation is reflected in recent views of homosexuality. Wilson's (1978) sociobiological theory of sexuality includes homosexuality as necessary for species preservation. *The Diagnostic and Statistical Manual of Mental Disorders* (American Psychiatric Association 1980) no longer classifies homosexuality per se as a deviance. Recent findings of Bell and Weinberg (1978) reported that the "typical" homosexual did not exist; in their studies, homosexual lifestyles varied as much as heterosexual lifestyles. A recent survey of studies comparing homosexual and heterosexual orientations revealed the generally good life adjustment of the homosexual on a wide variety of personality characteristics (interview with D. Calderwood, Ph.D., late chairperson of the human sexuality program, New York University, December 1981).

Although theoretical views of homosexuality have changed, the study of bisexuality continues to pose difficult problems for researchers. Blumstein and Schwartz (1976) stated that there is "little coherent relationship between the amount and 'mix' of homosexual behavior in a person's biography and that person's choice to label themselves as bisexual, homosexual, or heterosexual" (p. 339). They found that some people with no homosexual experiences considered themselves bisexual, while others who had experiences with both sexes considered themselves exclusively homosexual or heterosexual.

According to Kinsey, confusion concerning labeling was reflected by the polarized concept of homosexuality and heterosexuality. To address these problems, he developed the Kinsey Heterosexual-Homosexual Scale (KHHS) (Kinsey et al. 1948). This scale is an equal interval scale with continuous gradations between heterosexuality and homosexuality. An individual rating was based on relative amounts of heterosexual and homosexual response. Kinsey used the scale to rate individuals on overt experiences and psychological reactions. The ratings are as follows:

(0)   Exclusively heterosexual.
(1)   Predominantly heterosexual, only incidentally homosexual.
(2)   Predominantly heterosexual, but more than incidentally homosexual.
(3)   Equally heterosexual and homosexual.
(4)   Predominantly homosexual, but more than incidentally heterosexual.
(5)   Predominantly homosexual, only incidentally heterosexual.
(6)   Exclusively homosexual.

In the Kinsey studies, 50 percent of males were exclusively heterosexual (0), 4 percent were exclusively homosexual (6), and the remaining 46 percent fell between 1 and 5 on the scale. While the scale displayed a less polarized view of sexual orientation, it failed to account for specific life situations, particularly those which changed over time. In this sense, the scheme still leads to labeling, viewing sexual orientation in a static fashion. Many recent studies (Saghir and Robbins 1973; Bell and Weinberg 1978; Masters and Johnson 1979) have used the Kinsey scale to classify the subject as "homosexual" or "heterosexual" and generally grouped the bisexuals with the homosexuals.

The difficulty of labeling a person on the basis of a Kinsey rating, without taking into consideration the dimensions of time or the multivariable aspects of sexual orientation (i.e., attraction, behavior, fantasy, lifestyle, emotional preference, social preference, self-identification), can be illustrated by the following examples. A married man who feels he is heterosexual is sexually involved with a male lover. A girl who breaks up with her male lover lives with a woman and then returns to the man. A woman who is in jail engages in sex with females for several years but returns to a heterosexual lifestyle once she is released. A teenager who has sex with his buddies in the locker room has sex with his girlfriend several hours later. A male nurse helps a male patient masturbate as part of the patient's rehabilitation.

Some recent research and theoretical writing have touched upon the multivariate aspect of sexual orientation and its importance in research. As De Cecco (1981) wrote: "To depict sexuality as fixed, bifurcated states of sexual orientation, and to ignore the fact that erotic preference is labile and interpenetrated by elements of physicality, emotion, and fantasy, is to impede and even to misdirect research" (p. 51). While they virtually ignored the continuum of the Kinsey scale, using it only to classify their sample as heterosexual or homosexual, Bell and Weinberg (1978) stated: "Before one can say very much about a person on the basis of his or her sexual orientation, one must make a comprehensive appraisal of the relationship among a host of features pertaining to the person's life" (p. 329). In their programmatic research, Shively, Rudolph, and De Cecco (1978) identified the sexual-orientation characteristics of physical sexual activity, interpersonal affection, and erotic fantasy on a Kinsey-type continuum.

The Klein Sexual Orientation Grid (Klein 1980) was developed to measure a person's sexual orientation as a dynamic multivariable process. The grid (see Figure 1) was designed to extend the scope of the Kinsey scale by including attraction, behavior, fantasy, social and emotional preferences, self-identification, and lifestyle. These characteristics are also measured in the past, present, and as an ideal. In the present study it was postulated that the individual's sexual orientation is composed of sexual and nonsexual variables which differ over time. By studying a large group of individuals, this study validated the theoretical model of sexual orientation as multivariate and dynamic.

Sample Characteristics

The sample used for the analysis consisted of persons who filled out the questionnaire (KSOG) which appeared in an article entitled, "Are You Sure You're Heterosexual? Or Homosexual? Or Even Bisexual?" in *Forum* magazine (Klein 1980). Of the questionnaires returned to *Forum*, 384 were usable for data analysis. Out of the 384 respondents, 351 had completed all of the questions. The

Figure 1

Klein Sexual Orientation Guide

7/2/95
ABRAHAM

Variable	Past	Present	Ideal
A. *Sexual Attraction*	1 3	2 4	0 3
B. *Sexual Behavior*	2 2	1 1	1 4
C. *Sexual Fantasies*	5 2	6 6	1 4
D. *Emotional Preference*	2 4	4 5	1 4
E. *Social Preference*	6 1	4 1 2	4
F. *Self Identification*	1 5	4 2 1	4
G. *Straight/Gay Lifestyle*	1 6	5 2 1	4

fact that the sample used in this study was not drawn at random places significant limitations on interpretation of the data. Further limitations occur as a result of selection bias since it is not known specifically how *Forum* [now *Penthouse Forum* — T.G.] readers differ from other social populations. Although demographic data other than age, sex, and sexual orientation were not collected, *Forum's* readership is, according to its advertising department, largely college-educated and employed as professionals or managers.

Of the 384 respondents, 213 were male and 171 were female. One hundred twenty-eight respondents identified themselves as heterosexual, 172 as bisexual, and 62 as homosexual. Twenty-two respondents did not fill out the self-identification section. For the 384 respondents the mean age was 28.2 years, the range from 14 to 72.

A Chi-square Test for Independent Samples (Siegel 1956) showed a significant relationship between the sex of the respondents and their self-identification (Chi-square = 12.4, 2 df, p < .01). The percentage of males who identified themselves as bisexual or homosexual was greater than that of females. To study the relationship between the respondents' ages and the two independent variables of sex and self-identification, a Two-way Uni-variate Component Analysis of Variance (Pinneau & Ault 1974) was utilized. Results indicated a significant difference between the ages of males and females. For this sample the mean or average age of the females was significantly lower than that of the males. Secondly, there was a significant relationship between the respondents' self-identification and their age. The mean age of heterosexuals was significantly less than the mean age of bisexuals, and the mean age of bisexuals was significantly greater than the mean age of homosexuals. Further component analysis showed that the mean age difference between male bisexuals and homosexuals was significantly greater than the mean age difference between female bisexuals and homosexuals.

Method

Respondents were asked to fill out the Klein Sexual Orientation Grid, which was developed as an extension of the Kinsey Heterosexual-Homosexual Scale. The grid is based on Klein's previous research and requires a subject to provide 21 ratings in a seven-by-three grid (see Figure 1). Each rating on the grid is made using the numbers 1 through 7 which correspond to the choice on the heterosexual-homosexual continuum. In addition, for each area of sexual orientation three ratings are chosen: one for the respondent's past, one for the present (defined as the preceding year), and one based on the individual's ideal choice.

The KSOG was administered with the following instructions:

A. Sexual Attraction

Here you (in Figure 2) will be choosing three numbers, one for each of three aspects of your life: your past, your present, and your ideal. Beginning with your past, ask yourself where you fit on this scale and select the number that best describes you. Write this

Figure 2

1	2	3	4	5	6	7

Other sex only	Other sex mostly	Other sex somewhat more	Both sexes equally	Same sex somewhat more	Same sex mostly	Same sex only

number in the corresponding box marked past on the line for Variable A (Sexual Attraction) on the grid. Now, looking at Figure 2 again, select a number that describes your present sexual attraction using one year as the time period you examine. For a number of people it is the same number; for others it is different. Write this number in the box marked present on the line for Variable A. Now ask yourself which number you would choose to be if it were a matter of volition. Remember there are no right or wrong numbers. When you finish writing this last number in the box marked Ideal for Variable A on the grid you should have completed the three boxes for variable A.

B. Sexual Behavior

Here we look at actual behavior as opposed to sexual attraction. With whom do you have sex?

Use the scale in Figure 2 to rate yourself. As with the previous scale, choose a number for past, present, and ideal sexual behavior, then enter the numbers on the grid, this time under Variable B.

C. Sexual Fantasies

The third variable is sexual fantasy. Whether they occur during masturbation, while daydreaming, as a part of our real lives or purely in our imaginations, fantasies provide insight.

Rate yourself on the scale, then enter the numbers on the grid.

Figure 3

1	2	3	4	5	6	7

| Hetero only | Hetero mostly | Hetero somewhat more | Hetero/ gay equally | Gay somewhat more | Gay mostly | Gay only |

D. Emotional Preference

Our emotions directly influence, if not define, the actual physical act of love. Ask yourself if you love and like only the opposite sex or if you are also emotionally close to the same sex.

Find out where you fit on the scale; rate yourself as with the other scales. Enter the numbers on the grid.

E. Social Preference

Though closely allied to emotional preference, social preference is often different. You may love only women but spend most of your social life with men. Some people, of all orientations, only socialize with their own sex, while others socialize with the opposite gender exclusively.

Where are you on the scale? Choose three numbers as you have on the other scales.

F. Self-Identification

Your sexual self-definition is a strong variable since self-image strongly affects our thoughts and actions. In several cases, a person's present and past self-identification differs markedly from their ideal. Choose three numbers on the scale marked Figure 3 and fill in the numbers on the grid.

G. Heterosexual/Homosexual Lifestyle

Some heterosexuals only have sex with the opposite sex but prefer to spend the majority of their time with gay people. On the other hand, homosexual or bisexual persons may prefer to live exclusively in the gay world, the heterosexual world, or even to live in both worlds. Lifestyle is the seventh variable of sexual orientation.

Where do you tend to spend time and with whom? Choose three numbers in Figure 3 as you have on the other scales and enter them on the grid.

Results

The Klein Sexual Orientation Grid consisted of 21 questions. The respondents answered each question, using a seven-point Likert-type linear scale with seven dimensions of sexual orientation and past, present, and ideal as columns, creating 21 response cells. To test for reliability of the scales, Cronbach Alpha Coefficients using the Kuder-Richardson Formula 20 were computed utilizing the methods outlined by Nunally (1967). Alpha may be interpreted as the average correlation of the profile considering the items in the entire grid or each scale as a random sample of all possible measures of the same concept. The reliability estimates of the entire grid were generally excellent. Reliability estimates for the seven dimensions of sexual orientation were not as consistently high as the estimates for the past, present, and ideal scales. If the hypothesis is that a person's sexual orientation is different between the past, present, and ideal, then this may account for the lower reliability estimates among the scales measuring the seven dimensions.

To test for inter-relationships among the grid variables, item-to-item correlations were computed using the procedures described by Nunally (1967) for the 21 response cells. Results of the item-to-item correlations were generally high except for the "present social preference" and "past social preference." The results suggest that a person's social preference was somewhat different from the other aspects of his or her sexual orientation.

Given the relatively high correlations among the various sexual orientation profile items, the question arises whether the different items were really measuring different dimensions of sexual orientation, or simply measuring the same dimension. One way to answer this question was to determine whether the respondent gave different responses to each of the profile questions, or tended to give the same response. Since the answers to the grid questions were ordinal in nature, a Friedman Two-Way Analysis of Variance by ranks was computed using the procedures outlined by Siegel (1956). Such an analysis takes on the look of a nonparametric one-way analysis of variance based on a randomized complete block design. The results indicated there was a significant difference between the average ranks of the 21 profile variables on the grid.

From a theoretical standpoint, the primary scales of interest are the past, present, and ideal, since it was hypothesized that a person's sexual orientation changes over time. To test whether there was a difference in the mean scale scores for the past, present, and ideal, a Hotelling T-Square Analysis was performed following the procedures outlined by Morrison (1967). Statistical analysis showed a significant difference between the three mean scale scores. Simultaneous multiple comparisons indicated a significant difference between the present scale and the past scale, but none between the ideal and present scales.

Relationships Between Variables

To study the relationships among the independent variables of sex, age, and self-label, and the three scales of past, present, and ideal, several statistical analyses were performed. A Canonical Correlation Analysis (Morrison 1967) indicated that the vast majority of the variance (70 percent) between the two sets of variables was accounted for primarily by the respondent's self-identification. The second canonical variate of age accounted for approximately 11 percent of the variance between the two sets of variables. This analysis also suggested that whether a respondent was male or female was more strongly related to his or her past and ideal sexual orientation than were the independent variables of age or self-label.

Another method for studying relationships among the independent variables and the responses to the questions of the KSOG was the Automatic Interaction Detection as outlined by Lingwood (1981). This statistical analysis was carried out using the respondent's mean scores for all 21 questions on the grid as the dependent variables, and sex, age, and self-label as independent variables. Again, the best predictor of a respondent's mean score was his or her self-identification. In this analysis, the first statistical subpopulations or subgroups formed were based on the respondent's self-identification (heterosexual, homosexual, bisexual). For the most part, the respondent's sex determined the next set of subpopulations, with the exception of the heterosexual subpopulation whose orientation seemed to depend more on the respondent's age than sex. The results of the Automatic Interaction Detection analysis supported the findings from the Canonical Correlation analysis that the primary variable accounting for a respondent's sexual orientation on the KSOG was his or her self-identification.

Since previous analyses showed that for the sample as a whole there was a significant difference between the respondent's past, present, and ideal sexual orientation, a Multivariate Profile Analysis was conducted to determine whether the mean profiles for the three different subgroups (heterosexual, homosexual, bisexual) had the same significant differences. A One-Way Multivariate Component Analysis was carried out using the methods outlined by Pinneau and Ault (1974). The results indicated a significant difference between the mean profiles for the three subgroups in terms of their change in sexual orientation in the past, present, and ideal as measured on the KSOG. A further Univariate Analysis of Variance Test (Morrison 1967) indicated there was a significant difference between heterosexuals, bisexuals, and homosexuals in their past, present, and ideal sexual orientation as measured on the KSOG.

To study the differences among the heterosexual, homosexual, and bisexual subgroups, a Hotelling T-Square Analysis was also performed (Morrison 1967). The results for the heterosexual subgroup indicated a change in response between the past, present, and ideal scales. The change from past to present was not significant, but the change from present to ideal was significant. The results for the bisexual subgroup were just the reverse. Again, there was a significant overall change from past to ideal and a significant change from past to present, although there was no significant difference between the present and ideal. For the homosexual subgroup not only was the overall change from past to ideal significant, but the mean score for the present scale was also significantly higher than the mean score for the past scale, and the mean scale score for the present scale was significantly higher than the mean scale score for the ideal scale.

The results indicated that on the KSOG bisexuals and homosexuals had significant increases in homosexuality from the past to present histories, whereas heterosexuals remained constant. Comparing the present and ideal profiles, bisexuals and heterosexuals showed significant increase in homosexuality as an ideal. Homosexuals, in contrast, significantly decreased in homosexuality from the present to the ideal. The overall change from the past to ideal for heterosexuals, bisexuals, and homosexuals indicated significant increases in homosexuality for all three subgroups.

Discussion

The data analysis encompassed several key considerations: (1) the importance of viewing sexual orientation as a process which often changes over time; (2) the importance of all seven variables on the Klein Sexual Orientation Grid in describing sexual orientation; and (3) the simplicity and inadequacy of "heterosexual," "bisexual," and "homosexual" in describing a person's sexual orientation.

Analysis of the data revealed that sexual orientation was not static for this sample. Contrary to the theoretical notion that one becomes fixated in childhood, the sexual orientations of the individuals in this study often changed remarkably over the period of their adult lives. All three of the self-identified groups became significantly more homosexually oriented over time.

Since the changes from the past time-frame to the present were significant, the assumption was made that the ideal represented future changes in the sample's sexual orientations. There was a significant trend in the direction of the bisexual norm with the heterosexuals moving toward a more homosexual orientation over their lifetimes, and homosexuals moving away from a homosexual orientation. One might assume that these changes over a person's lifespan would hold true for bisexuals and homosexuals only. In this study, however, heterosexuals also changed.

Until recently the factor of change in sexual orientation has been generally ignored. Learning takes on a stronger role than genetic and hereditary factors. Many are potentially capable of traveling over a large segment of the sexual orientation continuum.

Theories of sexual orientation for heterosexual men and women have postulated a homosexual period during early puberty. If one remained homosexual or bisexual it was often misrepresented as an arrested adolescent development. Our impressions of sexual orientation, obtained through hundreds of interviews over the past five years and other studies outlined in *The Journal of Homosexuality*, lead us to conclude that many heterosexual men and women do, in fact, experiment with homosexual behavior for the first time in later life, and thereafter some change their identification to bisexual or homosexual. Conversely, for some male and female homosexuals, such experimentation and change also occur in adulthood and lead to greater heterosexuality. Bisexual men and women not only experiment and change in adult life, but for some the changes remarkably range over the entire sexual continuum.

Alfred Kinsey was a pioneer in assessing sexual orientation as a continuous rather than discrete phenomenon. His studies, however, limited the scope of sexual orientation for the most part to behavior. In the KSOG, sexual orientation consists of several aspects. It becomes a multivariable concept comprised of three variables which directly describe the sexual self (attraction, fantasy, and behavior), three which describe aspects considered crucial to the composition of sexual orientation (emotional preference, social preference, and heterosexual or homosexual lifestyle), and also the variable of self-identification.

For example, two people with an overall average of "4" for the "present" are very different if one has the configuration 4-4-4-4-4-4-4, while the other has 2-1-3-6-7-5-4. With respect to labeling their sexual orientation, both would be considered bisexual as a "4" on the Kinsey scale (altered from 0-6 to 1-7 to conform with the standard of the KSOG). In actuality, we are talking about two people with extremely different outlooks, lifestyles, sexualities, and social and emotional preferences. Furthermore, both persons would surely have had very different pasts and very different orientation ideals.

The results of cross-tabulating a person's self-identification number (using the seven-part scale) with the self-label he or she gave showed the simplicity and inadequacy of labeling (heterosexual, bisexual, homosexual). A logical but arbitrary method of differentiating the three labels by the seven-part scale is to assign the number 1 or 2 to the label heterosexuality, 3, 4, or 5 to bisexuality, and 6 or 7 to homosexuality. On the scale, one-third of those people who labeled themselves bisexual did not fit into the categories 3, 4, or 5. For the past, 30 percent did not fit. In the ideal 22 percent did not fit. The labels of homosexuality and heterosexuality fit only in the time period of the present where 88 percent placed themselves into categories 6 and 7 or 1 and 2, respectively. The label for bisexuals and homosexuals was inadequate for the past time period. Interestingly, in the ideal time-frame, more bisexuals than heterosexuals fit their numbered category (77 percent vs. 75 percent) while only 66 percent of homosexuals wished to remain ideally in their category.

Self-identified bisexuals had the lowest predictability overall; thus, the bisexual label did not predict well or label correctly. In the ideal, only the bisexuals remained the same as the present in retaining group membership, while the heterosexuals and homosexuals dropped substantially from their present percentages. Again, bisexuals wanted to remain ideally bisexual while the self-identified heterosexuals and homosexuals wanted to change toward the bisexual center of the continuum.

Although we suggest a word of caution regarding generalizing these findings to the overall population, we think that the Klein Sexual Orientation Grid proved to be a reliable and valid instrument in this study. (For validity and reliability statistics on the Klein Sexual Orientation Grid, refer to Wayson 1983.) We see the instrument as a useful tool in differentiating persons with respect to sexual orientation by taking into consideration the meaningful dimension of time and the many related variables. Describing the individual within this framework also allows the researcher to avoid the simplistic and inadequate labeling techniques which have undermined earlier studies of bisexuality.

We do not, at this point, have clear definitions of what constitutes a bisexual, homosexual, or heterosexual. This study has attempted to point out the pitfalls of conventional labeling. In his book, *Human Sexualities*, Gagnon (1977) stated:

> Whether we have expansive or narrow definitions of heterosexuality and homosexuality, love and lust, or clothed or naked sex, depends on the cultural significance that these dimensions have in both personal lives and the collective expressions of sexuality around us. Definitions should not be created to exhaust reality, to stand for all time or to account for all meanings in all circumstances. The utility of a definition is the direction it gives us for looking at the world. The definition should not be confused with the world itself. (p.188)

The Klein Grid provides a framework for understanding sexual orientation on a theoretical level. On the practical level it enables the researcher to separate groups more precisely, to focus on the individual while noting some of the common configurations. In addition, this study directs a researcher to be more explicit in describing which aspects of sexuality and emotional/social preference are being considered as variables, and to use a multivariate design rather than a simple contrast of distinct groups.

References

American Psychiatric Association. 1980. *Diagnostic and statistical manual of mental disorders*. 3d ed. Washington, D.C.: A.P.A.

Bell, A.P., and M.S. Weinberg. 1978. *Homosexualities: a study of diversity among men and women*. New York: Simon & Schuster.

Bieber, I. 1976. A discussion of "homosexuality": The ethical challenges. *Journal of Consulting and Clinical Psychology* 44: 163-166.

Blumstein, P.W., and P. Schwartz. 1976. Bisexuality in men. *Urban Life* 5: 339-358.

De Cecco, J.P. 1981. Definition and meaning of sexual orientation. *Journal of Homosexuality* 6 (4): 51-67.

Ellis, A. 1965. *Homosexuality: its causes and cures*. New York: Lyle Stuart.

Freud, A. 1971. *Problems of psychoanalytic training, diagnosis and techniques of therapy*. Vol. 7. London: International University Press.

Freud, S. 1910. Three contributions to sexual theory. *New York Journal of Nervous and Mental Disorders* 7: 472-474.

———— 1961. Three essays on the theory of sexuality. *The standard edition of the complete psychological works of Sigmund Freud* Vol. 7. Edited and translated by J. Strachey. London: Hogarth Press. (Original work published 1905.)

Gagnon, J. 1977. *Human Sexualities*. Glenview, IL: Scott, Foresman.

Hooker, E. 1969. Parental relations and male homosexuality in patient and non-patient samples. *Journal of Counseling and Clinical Psychology* 33: 141-142.

Kinsey, A. C., W. B. Pomeroy, and C. E. Martin. 1948. *Sexual Behavior in the human male*. Philadelphia: W.B. Saunders.

Klein, F. 1978. *The bisexual option*. New York: Arbor House.

———— 1980. Are you sure you're heterosexual? or homosexual? or even bisexual? *Forum*, Dec., 41-45.

Krafft-Ebing, R. von. 1965. *Psychopathia sexualis*. Translated from the German by F. S. Klaf. Briarcliff Manor, N.Y.: Stein and Day. (Original 12th edition published 1912.)

Lingwood, D. A. 1981. *Automatic interaction detection*. Washington D.C.: Action Research Northwest.

Masters, W.H., and V. E. Johnson. 1979. *Homosexuality in perspective.* Boston: Little, Brown.

Mead, M. 1975. Bisexuality: What's it all about? *Redbook Magazine,* Jan.

Morrison, D.F. 1967. *Multivariate statistical methods.* New York: McGraw-Hill.

Nunally, J.C. 1967. *Psychometric theory.* New York: McGraw-Hill.

Pinneau, S., and J. Ault. 1974. Univariate and multivariate component analysis. *Perceptual and Motor Skills* 39: 955-985.

Saghir, M.T., and E. Robbins. 1973. *Male and female homosexuality: A comprehensive investigation.* Baltimore: Williams & Wilkins.

Shively, M., J. Rudolph, and J. P. De Cecco. 1978. The identification of the social sex-role stereotypes. *Journal of Homosexuality* 3: 225-233.

Siegel, S. 1956. *Nonparametric statistics for the behavioral sciences.* New York: McGraw-Hill.

Wayson, P. 1983. A study of personality variables in males as they relate to differences in sexual orientation. Ph.D. diss., California School of Professional Psychology, San Diego.

Wilson, E. O. 1978. *On human nature.* Boston: Harvard University Press.

Editor's note: The following excerpt deals mostly with extremes of atypical gender differentiation, particularly as is developed in the prenatal stage; the authors call these atypical developments "errors." In the opinion of this editor, however, it is not useful to think of these atypical developments as "errors," (a judgmental term which suggests a need for correction), but rather as deviances from the norm, which can be welcomed or despised as the affected person prefers. It is also useful to note that certain gender-determining, biological features (such as sex hormone levels) differ from person to person, making it impossible to determine what is "perfect" for a man or a woman.

Much of the study that is done on homo- and bi-sexuality is done from a sociological point of view: indeed, most of the writings in this volume are sociological in perspective (Ms. Udis-Kessler's essay on constructionism vs. essentialism, for example). These writings tend to favor the belief that one's environment and personal choices are the determining factors of sexuality. The article below is from a more biological point of view and, as such, favors the belief that gender and sexuality are more biologically determined, out of the control of the individual, and largely settled before birth.

Normal and Atypical Gender Differentiation
by Albert Richard Allgeier, Ph.D., and Elizabeth Rice Allgeier, Ph.D.

From their book *Sexual Interactions*. 2d ed. Lexington, Massachusetts: D.C. Heath and Company, ©1988.

The process by which we become either male or female occurs in a series of stages during the development of the embryo and fetus. Although the steps in this process are usually predictable, errors occasionally occur. We will first look at the normal process.

Normal Gender Differentiation

In this section we will examine the process of gender differentiation as it affects the development of gonads and external genitals and the production of hormones. Differentiation begins with the establishment of genetic gender at conception and continues until the twelfth or thirteenth week of pregnancy.

Gonadal Gender

At eight weeks the embryo, whether it is genetically male (XY) or female (XX), has a pair of gonads and the beginnings of external genitals. It contains tissue that may eventually form female structures such as the fallopian tubes, the uterus, and the upper part of the vagina; this tissue is called the *Müllerian duct system*. The lower two-thirds of the vagina forms from the same tissue that gives rise to the urinary bladder and urethra — the urogenital sinus. It also contains tissue that may form male structures such as the epididymis, vas deferens, seminal vesicles, and ejaculatory duct; this tissue is called the *Wolffian duct system* (see figure 1). How these structures begin to develop into either male or female reproductive systems is not completely understood. The presence of a Y chromosome, however, appears to speed up cell division (Mittwoch 1973). For a number of years, researchers have believed that a gene or genes on the Y chromosome cause the formation of the H-Y antigen, a substance that causes the inner part of the gonads to begin developing the tubular structures of testes (Haseltine & Ohnos 1981). Recent evidence has narrowed down the location of the testes-determining factor to the short arm of the Y chromosome (Kolata 1986). If there is not a Y chromosome to issue these instructions, the embryo continues to grow for another few weeks before the outer part of the primitive gonads develops into ovaries packed with egg cells.

Hormonal Gender

The early development of the testes appears to be related to another embryonic phenomenon that provides a clue to how the process of gender differentiation works. If the gonads are removed during the critical embryonic period, the embryo will develop as a female, even if it is genetically male (XY). Therefore, as Money and

Figure 1

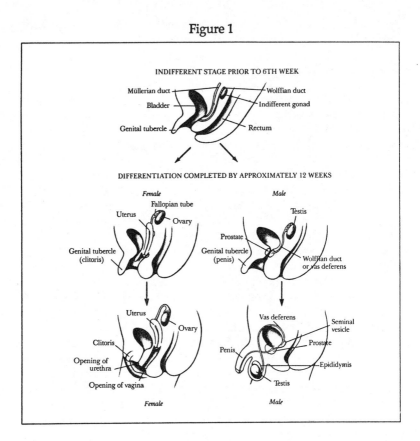

INDIFFERENT STAGE PRIOR TO 6TH WEEK

Müllerian duct — Wolffian duct
Bladder — Indifferent gonad
Genital tubercle — Rectum

DIFFERENTIATION COMPLETED BY APPROXIMATELY 12 WEEKS

Female — *Male*

Fallopian tube
Uterus — Ovary — Testis
Prostate
Genital tubercle (clitoris) — Genital tubercle (penis) — Wolffian duct or vas deferens

Uterus — Ovary — Vas deferens — Seminal vesicle
Clitoris — Penis — Prostate
Opening of urethra — Epididymis
Opening of vagina — Testis

Female — *Male*

Ehrhardt (1972) put it, "Nature's rule is, it would appear, that to masculinize, something must be added."(P. 7) This extra something that must be added consists of testosterone and Müllerian-inhibiting substance (MIS), a protein hormone. When the primitive gonads differentiate as testes in the male, they begin to manufacture these two substances.

Testosterone promotes the development of the Wolffian ducts to form the internal male reproductive structures. MIS, the chemical makeup of which is not completely known, is responsible for curbing the growth of the Müllerian duct system. Both of these substances must be present for normal development of the internal reproductive structures of the male. In normal development, then, only one of the duct systems expands and develops. The development of the other system is inhibited, so only rudimentary traces remain in the body.

Because of the popular definition of androgens as male hormones and estrogens as female hormones, many people mistakenly assume that we produce one or the other, depending on whether we are male or female. In fact, both genders secrete the same three types of hormones. In males, the testes synthesize progesterone (one of a general class of feminizing hormones called progestins), testosterone (an androgen), and estradiol (an estrogen). Similarly, in females, the ovaries secrete progesterone, androgens, and estrogen. Both genders also secrete small amounts of all these hormones from the cortex of their adrenal glands.

Gender differentiation depends on the mixture of these hormones in much the same way as the products of one's baking depends on the mixture of flour, sugar, baking powder, eggs, salt, and milk. Just as cake is created with larger proportions of sugar and eggs, and bread results from higher proportions of flour and salt, gender is influenced by the relative proportions of androgens and estrogens secreted. The proportion of androgens and estrogens varies somewhat within individuals; a difference in proportions, as long as it is within normal limits, does not seem to affect the individual's gender or sexual functioning. The effects of differences in the levels of masculinizing and feminizing hormones on the developing brain are a subject of controversy.

To form a rough idea of the importance of the hormonal mix for gender differentiation, consider that the testosterone level in male fetuses between the critical twelfth and seventeenth weeks of pregnancy is about 10 times the level found in female fetuses and about equal to the level found in adult males (Lev-Ran 1977). The level of testosterone begins to decline after about the seventeenth week. Testosterone concentrations in male fetuses are identical to those in female fetuses by the seventh month and remain so until puberty (Vermeulen 1986).

Genital Gender

Several weeks after the internal structures of the embryo have differentiated, with one set of potential reproductive organs beginning to develop and the other set beginning to atrophy, the external genitals begin to differentiate. Our external genitals are created from a small, protruding bud of tissue called a *genital tubercle*, and opening with a small swelling called the *labioscrotal swelling*, and folds or strips of skin called *urogenital folds* on each side of the tubercle (Wilson, George & Griffin 1981). (See figure 2.) If testes are developing, testosterone begins circulating in the bloodstream. As we have seen, testosterone acts directly on the Wolffian ducts to cause differentiation of the vas deferens, epididymis, and seminal vesicles. For the development of the external male genitals, however, testosterone is converted to a more potent product, *dihydrotestosterone* (DHT). DHT causes the elongation of the genital tubercle into the phallus. As the phallus grows, it pulls the urogenital folds forward, and they fuse with each other on the underside of the penis to form a urethral tube. The urethral tube connects to the bladder, prostate gland, and vas deferens. The two labioscrotal swellings fuse together to form a scrotum, which houses the testes when they eventually descend from the abdominal cavity, about eight months after conception.

The development of female external genitals needs no hormonal prompting — it occurs in the absence of male hormones. In females, the genital tubercle remains relatively small and becomes a clitoris. Instead of fusing, the urogenital folds of skin remain distinct and form the two inner lips of the vulva (labia minora) and the clitoral hood. The two labioscrotal swellings also remain separate, forming the two outer vaginal lips (the labia majora). The opening develops a dividing wall of tissue that separates the vaginal entrance to the uterus from the urethra, which connects to the bladder.

Figure 2

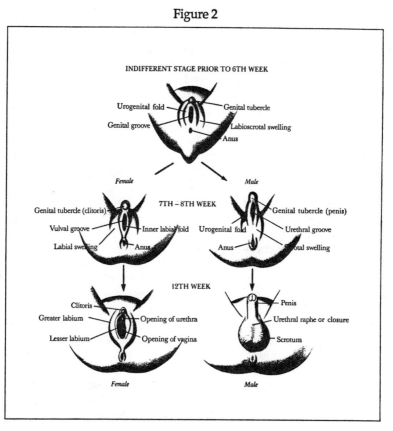

INDIFFERENT STAGE PRIOR TO 6TH WEEK

Urogenital fold — — Genital tubercle

Genital groove — — Labioscrotal swelling

— Anus

Female   *Male*

7TH – 8TH WEEK

Genital tubercle (clitoris) — — Genital tubercle (penis)

Vulval groove — — Inner labial fold   Urogenital fold — — Urethral groove

Labial swelling — Anus   Anus — Scrotal swelling

12TH WEEK

Clitoris — — Penis

Greater labium — — Urethral raphe or closure

Lesser labium — — Opening of urethra — Scrotum

— Opening of vagina

Female   *Male*

Atypical Gender Differentiation

Errors in the process of gender differentiation , although rare, can occur at any stage of development. Abnormalities can be caused by inheritance of atypical sex chromosomes, by abnormal differentiation of gonads, or by alterations in the secretion of sex hormones.

Sex Chromosome Abnormalities

Chromosomal abnormalities may occur in either the autosomal (body) chromosomes or the sex chromosomes. Although defects in the autosomes such as Down's syndrome can also affect gender and sexual development, we will focus on abnormalities in the sex chromosomes. So far, more that 70 irregularities of the sex chromosomes have been identified (de la Chapelle 1983). Many of these are caused by abnormal combinations of sex chromosomes that cause a person to be neither an XX female nor an XY male. Some of the more common sex chromosome abnormalities are presented in Table 1.

Atypical chromosome patterns occur in approximately 1 out of every 100 to 200 people (Diamond 1978). Identification of such patterns has been invaluable in helping to explain the influence of the sex chromosomes.

The X chromosome appears to be crucial for survival. No one has ever been born with only a Y chromosome (YO), probably because of the relative paucity of genetic information carried by the Y. The genes of the Y chromosome are coded for "maleness" and little else. The presence of a single Y chromosome generally results in an individual's having a male appearance, no matter how many X chromosomes that individual happens to have in his chromosomal makeup. Feminine development can occur without the presence of a second X, as in Turner's syndrome. The absence of a second X, however, reduces the likelihood of ovarian development and fertility.

In general, extra X chromosomes do not enhance female characteristics, although they may make males more like females. Extra Y chromosomes, however, may produce exaggerated masculine physical qualities. In addition, extra X and Y chromosomes appear to be related to intelligence (Hoyenga & Hoyenga 1979). An extra Y is associated with reduced intelligence, although the intelligence of individuals with an extra Y chromosome is not as limited as that of individuals with extra X chromosomes. (Women who risk producing babies with atypical chromosomal patterns, either because of age or because of a history of giving birth to chromosomally atypi-

Table 1: Common Sex Chromosome Abnormalities

Syndrome	Make-up of Chromosomes	Incidence per Live Births	Characteristics	Treatment
Klinefelter's syndrome	X X Y; in rare cases, an extra X occurs (X X X Y)	1 in 1,000	Shrunken testes, breast development (gynecomastia) in about 1/2 of all cases, disproportionate arms and legs, elevated urinary gonadotropins, infertility in most cases, low levels of testosterone sometimes, increased likelihood of mental retardation.	Administration of testosterone during adolescence often produces more masculine body contours and sexual characteristics as well as increasing sex drive.
XYY syndrome	X Y Y	1 in 1,000	Genital irregularities, decreased fertility, increased likelihood of mental retardation.	
Turner's syndrome	X O	1 in 3,000*	Short stature (4 to 5 feet), loose or weblike skin around the neck, a broad and "shield-like" chest with the nipples widely spaced, nonfunctional ovaries, no menstruation or development of adult breasts, infertility in almost all cases.	Administration of estrogen and progesterone can induce menstruation and development of the breasts, external genitals, and pubic hair. Androgen administered during puberty can help the child attain a greater adult height.
Triple-X syndrome	X X X	1 in 1,000	Most of these women show no major abnormalities, though they are likely to be less fertile than XX females; higher incidence of mental disturbance than among XX females.	

* This figure is not an accurate indicator of this condition. About 1/10 of all pregnancies that end in spontaneous abortion are XO — although this is a conservative estimate given that many embryos with Turner's syndrome and other atypical chromosomal patterns are spontaneously aborted, at times before the woman is even aware she is pregnant.

cal babies, can undergo chorionic villi sampling or amniocentesis.)

Inconsistencies in Prenatal Gender Differentiation

In addition to atypical sex chromosome patterns, another cause of atypical gender differentiation is an error in the process of gender differentiation during prenatal development. A discrepancy may occur between genetic gender and gonadal, hormonal, or genital gender. An inconsistency in the process of prenatal gender differentiation results in a condition known as *intersexuality* or *hermaphroditism*.

The word *hermaphrodite* comes from the names of the Greek god and goddess of love, Hermes and Aphrodite. Their union was thought to have produced a god having characteristics of both genders. (The word itself suggests a dual-gendered creature capable of impregnating itself, but to date no instance of a human capable of self-impregnation has ever been verified.) The term is used to refer to an infant born with abnormal anatomical development.

True hermaphrodites, possessing both ovarian and testicular tissue, are exceedingly rare. In about 33 percent of the known cases of hermaphroditism, the person has an ovary on one side (usually the left) and a testis on the other. In another 20 percent of the cases, *ovatestes* appear. Ovatestes are undifferentiated gonads — that is, gonads that didn't develop into either testes or ovaries. Finally, in some cases the person has an ovatestis on one side and either a testis or an ovary on the other (Simpson 1983).

Hermaphrodites are usually genetic females, in spite of the presence of testes or other male anatomical features. In almost all cases a uterus is present, but the external genitals can vary considerably. Because the phallus is generally enlarged, two-thirds of true hermaphrodites are raised as males (Lev-Ran 1977). Complications arise when a true hermaphrodite, assigned the male gender at birth, begins at puberty to develop breasts and to menstruate, as a result of the secretion of estrogens from the previously unsuspected ovaries. The cause of hermaphroditism is still not understood.

Most types of atypical gender differentiation fall in the category of *pseudohermaphroditism*. Male pseudohermaphrodites are individuals whose external genitals fail to develop as expected for normal males. Similarly, female pseudohermaphrodites are individuals whose external genitals fail to develop as expected for normal females.

Gender Differentiation in Genetic Males

We will briefly examine some of the conditions that can lead to problems in gender differentiation in males. As we have seen, hormones are important in the development of early gender differentiation. Thus it would appear reasonable to assume that atypical patterns of exposure to sex hormones might lead to atypical gender differentiation. A number of researchers have investigated this hypothesis.

Androgen Exposure: Exposure of genetic males to excess levels of androgen during prenatal development appears to have no effect on the development of their internal or external genitals. Exposure to excess androgen may, however, have some effect on behavior. Ehrhardt (1975) compared nine boys who were prenatally exposed to higher-than-normal levels of androgens with their unaffected siblings. The androgen-exposed boys differed from their brothers only in their greater interest in sports and rough activities.

Exposure to higher-than-normal levels of estrogen during the prenatal period does not appear to produce any degree of anatomical abnormality in either gender (Ehrhardt et al. 1984; Reinisch 1977). In experiments with mammals, this exposure does, however, appear to result in the demasculinization of the genitals and more "feminine" behavior (Ehrhardt & Meyer-Bahlburg 1981). These studies, in which both males and females who experienced increased prenatal exposure to estrogen were compared with others in appropriate control groups, indicate that such exposure might be related to somewhat more stereotypical female behaviors. Prenatal exposure of males to higher progesterone levels does not affect anatomical development and has little effect on the gender-related behavior of young boys (Ehrhardt et al. 1984; Kester 1984).

Androgen Insensitivity Syndrome: Some XY people have a condition known as androgen insensitivity syndrome (AIS, sometimes called testicular feminization), in which the body secretes normal amounts of androgen but the body cells are unresponsive to androgen (Money & Ehrhardt 1972). This condition is thought to be the result of an X-linked recessive trait, which is transmitted by females but affects only their male offspring.

The Wolffian structures of an AIS fetus fail to develop into normal internal male structures (prostate, seminal vesicles, and vas deferens) because they are insensitive to androgen. The Müllerian-inhibiting substance, however, usually transmits its instructions, so the Müllerian structures do not develop either. Thus the fetus is born without a complete set of either male or female internal genital organs.

AIS individuals develop a normal clitoris and a short vagina. The vagina generally does not lead to a functional uterus, but occasionally a small structure regarded as a rudimentary uterus is present. Testes do not usually descend; if they do, they appear only as small lumps near the labia. These small lumps are often misdiagnosed as hernias. The undescended gonads (testes) don't produce viable sperm. Because people with this syndrome do respond to the presence of female hormones, breast development and female pelvic changes occur at the onset of puberty. Menstruation does not occur, and the person with AIS cannot reproduce.

Sexual activity and orgasm can occur in AIS people. Since their genitals appear to be female, they are typically raised as females from birth, and they develop female gender identities. Minor surgery is sometimes needed to lengthen the upper vagina for satisfactory sexual intercourse. If testes are discovered, they are generally surgically removed during childhood or adolescence, because leaving the testes in place increases the risk of cancer. These individuals are then given estrogen supplements to replace the estrogen formerly secreted by the testes.

John Money and his colleagues studied 14 AIS people who were raised as females. In attitude and behavior, these people resembled traditional females, exhibiting well-developed maternal desire. The research group described them as excellent adoptive mothers (Money & Ehrhardt 1972; Money, Ehrhardt & Masica 1968). Because they were socialized as females, it is difficult to separate the effects of their insensitivity to androgen from the effects of their being raised as females.

Occasionally, an AIS individual will have a phallus large enough to cause him to be identified as a male at birth. When he reaches puberty, however, he begins to develop breasts, and he totally lacks masculine body traits. His penis may not have the ability to become erect, and his prostate gland may not produce ejaculatory fluid. Surgery can complete the fusion of his scrotum and bring his sterile testes down into it, but it cannot make his penis grow. His pubescent breasts can be surgically removed, but masculine secondary sexual characteristics cannot be created. Giving him extra doses of testosterone is useless: he is producing all that he needs, but his body cells cannot make use of it. AIS individuals tend to have bodies that appear female, and they have difficult sex lives.

Borderline Androgen Insensitivity Syndrome: Individuals with a condition known as borderline androgen insensitivity syndrome can make partial use of testosterone. The infant is born with a "penis" only slightly larger than a clitoris, and he lacks an urethra. His scrotum is partially unfused, and the testes can be felt as lumps in the groin. The best solution for this child is to be raised as a female. Surgery can reduce the size of the penis and separate the scrotum to open and deepen the vagina. Female hormones (estrogen) can be administered to produce the development of breasts and other female characteristics. For the individual with AIS, then, the possession of an XY chromosome pattern and testes doesn't always mean being "male."

DHT Deficiency Syndrome: DHT deficiency syndrome is a genetic disorder that prevents the prenatal conversion of testosterone into DHT. Males suffering from DHT deficiency syndrome lack an enzyme (5α reductase) necessary for this conversion (Imperato-McGinley et al. 1974). As described earlier, DHT stimulates the development of the external male genitals. Thus at birth males with DHT deficiency do not have identifiably male genitals.

Several cases of DHT deficiency syndrome were discovered in an isolated village in the Dominican Republic. Researchers studied 33 genetically male inhabitants of the village who had the enzyme deficiency. At birth these males had genitals that either were ambiguous or resembled those of females. At puberty, however, they experienced an increase in muscle mass, growth of the phallus and scrotum, and deepening of the voice. Nineteen of the males studied by the researchers had been raised as females up to the age of puberty. Of these, adequate information could be obtained on eighteen. Sixteen of the eighteen gradually adopted a masculine gender identity and erotic interest in women. One of the remaining two changed his gender identity but continued to dress and live as a woman; erotically, he behaved and felt like a heterosexual man, adopting a pattern resembling that of male transvestites. The other retained a feminine gender identity and role, marrying a man at age 16. These findings suggest that pseudohermaphrodites, although basically male, can adopt a feminine identity and gender role if raised as females during childhood. Their gender identity and role can be overturned at a later age — at least in the Dominican culture — if secondary sex characteristics of the other gender emerge.

Genetic Differentiation in Genetic Females

Prenatal exposure to excess androgen has the effect of masculinizing genetic females. Three sources of such masculinization have been identified: (1) malfunction of fetal adrenal glands, (2) administration of hormones to pregnant women, and (3) ovarian tumors during pregnancy.

Androgenital Syndrome: Androgenital syndrome (AGS), also known as *congenital adrenal hyperplasia*, is a genetically transmitted malfunction of the adrenal glands. A fetus with this condition secretes too much androgen. Normally, the adrenal glands secrete both cortisol (related to levels of androgens in the body) and androgens. The adrenal glands of AGS XX females, however, fail to synthesize cortisol, and instead secrete excess androgens (Freund 1985).*

The release of extra androgens during the critical period for differentiation of the external genitals (about three months after conception) leads to masculinization of the external genitals. If it is realized at birth that the masculinized baby is really a female, her external genitals can be surgically changed shortly after birth. In addition, she can be given synthetic cortisol (cortisone) to reduce the output of androgens from the adrenal glands. Under these conditions, the child will develop normally, experience the typical further gender differentiation associated with puberty, and be a sexually and reproductively normal female.

If the problem is not corrected by cortisone injections from infancy onward, the excess androgen secretion will continue to masculinize the child after birth and at puberty.

Changes in Maternal Hormone Levels: Masculinization of the external genitals of genetic females may also result from the mother's having received hormones called progestogens during pregnancy (Money & Ehrhardt 1972). Progestogens — synthetic progestins that are chemically related to testosterone — were at one time given to women who were at risk of miscarriage, to help them maintain their pregnancies. Follow-up studies of baby girls born to women who took progestogens during their pregnancies have shown that the masculinizing effects of the hormones were limited to the prenatal period. Once the babies were born, the masculinizing influence of the hormones ended.

At birth, the appearance of babies affected by progestogens varied, depending on the strength of the masculinizing hormone — some looked female, some looked male, and some looked ambiguous. Their internal reproductive organs, however, devel-

---

* Males are as likely to inherit AGS as are females. The syndrome usually is not detected until about five years of age when, due to the high level of androgens in the body, the child experiences a sudden growth spurt.

oped normally. Thus those babies who were recognized as females and given adequate surgical and hormonal treatment developed normally and were capable of reproduction.

The fate of genetic females with progestin-induced masculinized external genitals provides a good example of the interaction of biological, psychological, and social factors in the formation of gender identity. When the effect of the progestin is pronounced, females may be born with a clitoris the size of a penis and with labia that have fused to give the appearance of a scrotum. The "penis" may even contain the urethral tube. When these females are born, the pronouncement "It's a boy" is quite understandable. (The fact that the child's "scrotum" is empty wouldn't necessarily raise questions because in two percent of all males the testes don't descend into the scrotum until after birth.) At puberty, however, the child's ovaries secrete normal amounts of estrogen, which elicits menarche (first menstruation) and the beginnings of female body contours. By this time, of course, the genetic female has lived a dozen or so years under the assumption that she is a male, and the discovery of her internal femininity, not to mention the enlargement of breasts, can be a shock. After all this time with a male gender identity, the person may choose to have the female internal organs (ovaries and uterus) removed surgically. Administration of androgen will help to masculinize the body and artificial testes can be inserted into the scrotum, but no sperm will be produced.

Assigned Gender vs. Genetic Gender: An intriguing comparison was made by Money and Ehrhardt (1972) among genetic females with (1) progestin-induced masculinization, (2) androgenital syndrome (AGS), and (3) normal sexual differentiation. Individuals in all three groups were perceived as female at birth and were raised with no ambiguity regarding their gender. The ten girls in the first group were exposed to progestin prenatally but to no masculinizing agents after birth. The 15 girls in the second group were immediately recognized as having AGS and placed on cortisone therapy to correct the condition.

Comparisons of the childhood behavior of the girls in the first two groups with that of the 25 normal girls in the third group indicated that the prenatally masculinized girls were more likely to display a number of stereotypically male interests and behaviors while developing a female gender identity. They liked strenuous physical activity and were not very concerned about "feminine" attire. They tended to join boys in rough games such as football. Girls in the first two groups were more likely to be described as tomboys throughout their childhood. Although some of the girls in the normal control group also engaged in episodes of tomboyish behavior, which is typical for most girls in our culture, the consistency of the behavior in the first two groups led Money and Ehrhardt to speculate that the "male" childhood behavior was linked to the presence of progestin or androgen during prenatal development. The behavioral differences between the AGS girls and the normal girls could be due to genetic factors or could result from some alteration in the uterine environment other than excess androgen. The girls who were prenatally masculinized by the artificial progestins, however, showed many of the same masculine childhood behaviors.

Dosage level appears to be a crucial factor in the effect of progestin. With the use of lower doses of progestin, the masculinizing effect seen in the Money and Ehrhardt study does not appear (Freund 1985). Ehrhardt et al. (1984) reported that young girls who had been exposed to progestin prenatally exhibited slightly *more* female-stereotyped behavior than did normal girls. In experiments with monkeys, testosterone has been observed to have a masculinizing effect. The period of gestation, or prenatal development, for a rhesus monkey is 168 days. Testosterone administration prior to 40 days aborts the fetus. Injection of testosterone into the pregnant mother between days 40 and 134 of the the pregnancy partially masculinizes the genitals of XX monkeys (Goy & Phoenix 1971). The genetically female monkeys usually developed a small but well-formed penis with a urethral opening at its tip and a well-developed but empty scrotum. These monkeys retained their internal female structures, which developed because there was no Müllerian-inhibiting substance to prevent their development.

Although they did not attain the level of activity of normal males, the testosterone-treated infant female monkeys engaged in more activity — wrestling, chasing, and threatening or pseudo-aggressive behaviors — than did untreated females. This difference may have been due to differential treatment they received from other monkeys as a result of their masculine appearance rather than to fetal testosterone exposure. We know that testes are not necessary for normal male social play during the first two years, however, because males who are castrated at birth are indistinguishable from normal males in their social play behavior up until the end of their second year. Similarly, removing the ovaries from otherwise normal female rhesus monkeys does not alter their social play.

Presumably, then, this difference is the result of the presence of testosterone during the fetal period. With the addition of testosterone, the brain is biased in the male direction, even if that brain belongs to a genetic female.

The effects of excess estrogen on human genetic females are not clear. There appears to be no effects on their genitals. Although some increases in stereotypically female behavior have been observed among estrogen-exposed girls, the extent to which this behavior was due to prenatal estrogen exposure is not known (Ehrhardt & Meyer-Bahlburg 1981).

Gender Differentiation and Gender Identity

The preceding overview of the disorders associated with atypical hormone exposure suggests two important conclusions. First, the sex hormones, particularly androgens, have enormous influence on anatomical differentiation in a male or female direction during prenatal development.

Given the dramatic effects of the presence or absence of androgens on the internal and external genitals, the second conclusion is even more remarkable: gender assignment and socialization — being raised as a boy or a girl — often has more of an impact on gender identity — the psychological sense of being male or female — than does one's genetic (XX or XY) gender. Thus when an anatomical error is discovered in infancy and is corrected, gender identity will tend to be consistent with genetic gender. When an error is not discovered until puberty or later, however, gender identity is often more important for self-concept than is genetic gender. In these cases, surgical and hormonal treatments are generally more successful when their goal is to make anatomical (genital) gender consistent with gender identity rather than with genetic gender (Money & Ehrhardt 1972).

The experience of the DHT-deficient males in the Dominican Republic, most of whom successfully changed their gender identity with the onset of puberty and the development of secondary sexual characteristics, is a notable exception to the general rule that by puberty gender identity is more important than is genetic gender. This exception could be due to the prenatal effects of androgen on the boys' brains. As mentioned earlier, there is increasing evidence that androgens may masculinize the brain. The lack of DHT, which affected their external genitals, would not have altered their response to prenatal androgens. Perhaps their brains were masculinized prenatally, enabling them to make a smooth transition from female to male identity at puberty.

References

de la Chapelle, A. 1983. Sex chromosome abnormalities. In *Principles and practices of medical genetics*, ed. A.E. Emery and D.L. Rimorin, 193-215. New York: Churchill Livingstone.

Diamond, M. 1978. Human sexual development: Biological foundations for social development. In *Human sexuality in four perspectives*, ed. F. Beach, 22-61. Baltimore: The Johns Hopkins University Press.

Ehrhardt, A.A. 1975. Prenatal hormone exposure and psychosexual differentiation. In *Topics in psychoendocrinology*, ed. E.J. Sacher, 67-82. New York: Grune & Stratton.

Ehrhardt, A.A., and H.F.L. Meyer-Bahlburg. 1981. Effects of prenatal sex hormones on gender-related behavior. *Science* 211: 1312-1318.

Ehrhardt, A.A., H.F.L. Meyer-Bahlburg, J.L. Feldman, and S. Ince. 1984. Sex-dimorphic behavior in childhood subsequent to prenatal exposure to exogenous progesterones and estrogens. *Archives of Sexual Behavior* 13: 457-477.

Freund, K. 1985. Cross-gender identity in a broader context. In *Gender dysphoria: Development, research, management*, ed. B. W. Steiner, 259-324. New York: Plenum.

Goy, R.W., and C.H. Phoenix. 1971. The effects of testosterone propionate administered before birth on the development of behavior in genetic female rhesus monkeys. In *Steroid hormones and brain function*, ed. C. Sawyer and R.A. Gorski, 193-213. Berkeley: University of California Press.

Haseltine, F.P., and S. Ohnos. 1981. Mechanism of gonadal differentiation. *Science* 211: 1272-1278.

Hoyenga, K.B., and K.T. Hoyenga. 1979. *The question of sex differences.* Boston: Little, Brown.

Imperato-McGinley, J., L. Guerrero, T. Gautier, and R. Peterson. 1974. Seroid 5 reductase deficiency in man: An inherited form of male pseudohermaphroditism. *Science* 186: 1213-1215.

Kester, P. 1984. Effects of prenatally administered 17-hydroxyprogesteronecaproate on adolescent males. *Archives of Sexual Behavior* 13: 441-455.

Kolata, G. 1986. Maleness pinpointed on Y-chromosome. *Science* 234: 1076-1077.

Lev-Ran, A. 1977. Sex reversal as related to clinical syndromes in human beings. In *Handbook of sexology* Vol. 2, ed. J. Money and H. Musaph, 157-176. New York: Elsevier North Holland.

Mittwoch, U. 1973. *Genetics of sex differentiation.* New York: Academic Press.

Money, J., and A.A. Ehrhardt. 1972. *Man & woman, boy & girl.* Baltimore: Johns Hopkins University Press.

Money, J., A.A. Ehrhardt, and D.N. Masica. 1968. Fetal feminization induced by androgen insensitivity in the testicular feminizing syndrome: Effect on marriage and maternalism. *Johns Hopkins Medical Journal* 123: 105-114.

Reinisch, J.M. 1977. Prenatal exposure of human foetuses to synthetic progestin and oestrogen affects personality. *Nature* 266: 561-562.

Simpson, J.L. 1983. Disorders of gonads and internal reproductive ducts. In *Principles and practices of modern genetics* Vol. 2, ed. A. E. Emery and D.L. Rimorin, 1227-1240. New York: Churchill Livingstone.

Vermeulen, A. 1986. Leydig cell physiology. In *Male reproductive dysfunction,* ed R.J. Santen and R.S. Swerdloff, 49-76. New York: Marcel Dekker. 1986

Wilson, J.D., F.W. George, and J. Griffin. 1981. The hormonal control of sexual development. *Science* 211: 1278-1284.

A
Bisexual
Catalog

Tidbits!

"The woman who most needs liberating is the woman in every man. The man who most needs liberating is the man in every woman."

Reverend William Sloane Coffin, Jr., quoted in Hello, I Love You! *by Jeanne paslé-green and Jim Haynes.*

"[Traditional] Marriage: A community consisting of a master, a mistress, and two slaves, making in all, two."

Ambrose Bierce, quoted in Open Marriage, *Nena and George O'Neill.*

"While I'm on the subject of language, I propose to ban one word from this column, if not from this paper: 'lifestyle.' Gay, heterosexual or bisexual, we are all living real lives, in all their comedy and tragedy, and not some 'lifestyle,' as though it were some passing fad inspired by the media. The word has become repulsive to me ever since I noticed that it was increasingly paired with 'perverted.' If anyone has a perverted lifestyle, it's Donald Trump."

"Betty Barcode" (pseudonym), whose column "Bilines" appears in the Rochester, New York gay newspaper, Empty Closet.

Bi-Lexicon
by The Editor

Some Alternatives to the Word "Bisexual"

One problem in trying to bring together people who are open to sleeping with either sex is that we are known by such a wide variety of labels — and, more often than not, we refuse to label ourselves and therefore fail to identify with the group known as "bisexual." Many objections have been raised to the use of that particular term, the most common being that it emphasizes two things that, paradoxically, bisexuals are the least likely to be involved with: the dualistic separation of male and female in society, and the physical implications of the suffix "-sexual."

As a result, many people say nothing — and the world, of course, assumes that they are heterosexual. In other words, if we fail to claim our own right to identity, it may be ascribed to us — probably incorrectly.

Personally, I believe first and foremost in the right to claim one's own identity and be recognized in terms of that identity: the right of each creature to name itself. So when I meet a man who calls himself straight, I know that he *is* straight — regardless of what he does. Too often I've heard things like, "Well, he's gay, he just doesn't know it yet," or, "She says she's a lesbian, but she's really bi."

Terms are, of course, desperately limited in describing the pastel wash of a person's space, especially when we consider context. For example, living in the conservative Midwestern city of Cincinnati, I think of myself as "that Commie Jew fag from New York" — and people seem to know just what I mean. In Greenwich Village, however, I am something quite different. In any case, none of those terms is really technically accurate: I'm not a follower of Communism, though I come from a tradition of leftist thinking and believe in collectivism; I was born with "Jewish blood," although my family hasn't practiced Judaism for three generations; I've only been sexually involved with a man once or twice; and I'm from a suburb of New York City, not the city itself. But the essence of what I am, and how I see myself, is better expressed in those concise few words than could be done in paragraphs. Anyhow, I'm not in the habit of speaking in paragraphs — are you?

And so below are a few of the more common terms of self-definition, and how they've come to be used. Also listed are some newer and more unusual ways of describing oneself in a few words.

Bisensual, Bigenderist: Used to show a recognition for the ability to be sensual, intimate, and close to both males and females. May or may not include genital sexuality. Are sometimes used to make the point that sex is not the most important thing in a particular person's "bisexual" life, or may be used to blur the perhaps illusory line between sexuality and sensuality.

As with the word *Bisexual*, they usually also imply that relations with gender minorities are possible. (See also *Bisexual* and *Pansexual*.) Bisensual can be used as either an adjective or a noun.

Bisexual: (Here's my stab at a definition, using gender-free pronouns.) A bisexual person is one who recognizes pir *capacity* for being sexually intimate with males and females, whether or not it is acted upon. A bisexual person may, in action, have only same-sex or other-sex partners, or may never have a partner — and yet that person is bisexual if s/he senses that the *possibility* for sexual relations with either of the two major sexes is there. (Unless, of course, s/he rejects that label for pirself.)

An important distinction to remember: the word bisexual *does not* imply any particular sort of lifestyle.

As with the word *Bisensual* (see above), bisexual usually also implies that relations with gender minorities are possible. Can be used as either an adjective or a noun.

Bisexual Lesbian: For many, the word lesbian has come to mean not only a sexual preference, but also a political and social stance. It states that, in a male-dominated world, women (or wimmin, if you prefer, or wommin, or wymyn) *must* come first. However, a person choosing this term for herself also realizes her attraction to or ability to enjoy intimate relations with men.

Bi-Lesbian Feminist: Similar to *Bisexual Lesbian*, but also indicates an involvement in the feminist community, more specifically the lesbian feminist community (which is slightly different from the feminist community at large).

Byke: From the word dyke, which was originally a derogatory term for a lesbian until lesbians "claimed" it and started to use it to define themselves. Usually connotes great pride and participation in the lesbian/gay community. Also serves to state solidarity with the women's community. (See also *Bisexual Lesbian*.)

Cousin: I was introduced to a lesbian by a gay friend in this way: "Tom, this is Mary. She's 'family.' Mary, this is Tom. He's a cousin." (See also *Family*.)

Family: A discreet term used by lesbians and gays to identify one another (i.e. "I think that cute guy who works at the art store is family."). But now that bisexuals are starting to get together and form a sort of extended family, why not also use this term among ourselves? (See also *Cousin*.)

Equal Opportunity Lover: One of the more up-beat and "cutesy" ways of thinking of yourself. Is sort of righteous and bi-affirming: suggesting, perhaps, "Isn't this the most fair way to be?" The Boston Bisexual Women's Network produced shirts with this phrase on it, incorporated into an eye-catching design.

Equal Opportunity Rejector: Anti-cutesy. Also very clearly makes a point: being bisexual does not mean that one lacks personal tastes!

Gay Bisexual: Can mean one of two things:
a) A bisexual (of either sex) who tends (sexually) towards gay, but recognizes potential for heterosexual relations, or

b) A bisexual (of either sex) who is active in the gay community, either socially or politically.

Women choosing this term may also be showing their solidarity with gay men; otherwise, the term *Bisexual Lesbian* is usually used.

Holly: Apparently, some of the women in the Seattle Bisexual Women's Network have taken to this term. This explanation, from Gary North (in *Bisexuality: News, Views, and Networking*, April 1988): "Why a holly? It was explained to me this way. Singer Holly Near was asked if she was lesbian or straight. Her answer was that she was Holly."

Strangely enough, it seems that an institution has grown out of what was originally meant to be a statement of individuality! The point she made, though, is clear: realizing that answers to such questions really don't mean anything, why not identify yourself in a way that means something? Once, at a University of Cincinnati Gay/Lesbian Alliance presentation, I introduced myself in a similar way. We were going around the room, giving our names and how we identified. The circle came to me, and I said: "My name is Tom. I'm a Taurus."

Pansensual: Pansensual is to pansexual as bisensual is to bisexual. See *Bisensual* and *Pansexual*.

Pansexual: Two definitions are floating around now-a-days:
a) One who recognizes that one's sexual capacities transcend humanity; that inanimate objects, animals, plants, and concepts can also be sexually exciting, or
b) One whose sexual interests include people who are gender minorities, i.e. not male or female. (See separate article on *Normal and Atypical Gender Differentiation*, page 82.)

Since the second of these definitions is usually implied by the word *Bisexual*, I think that the first is the more useful. Can be used as either a noun or an adjective.

Directory of Bisexual Special-Interest Groups

These groups generally aim to establish a bisexual identity and the freedom for all people to exercise sexual self-determination in a noncoercive way. They also provide discussion opportunities and some social activities for people who are interested in bisexuality. Some groups are limited to women or men, as indicated in their names.

We have tried particularly to include excerpts from the statements we have received from those groups that seem to have programs that go beyond these basic activities.

A few notes from the editor:

1) First and foremost, this listing is ephemeral despite our efforts to keep it current. By the time this book is published, some of the groups listed below will have disappeared, while others will have sprung up. *Don't give up.* Addresses change, group facilitators change, but *the bisexual support network is here to stay.* Phone numbers are quite changeable, so I've chose to include them only for the most stable and best-known groups, except for those that list only phone numbers. Most of the others *do* publicize their phone numbers, so if you want a quicker contact than the mails afford, I'd suggest checking the lesbian/gay/alternative press in the group's area.

2) If you're unable to find a group that's listed here, there are a few things you can do:
a) Call the lesbian/gay helpline nearest to you. It is likely to know about area organizations, including bi groups. Lesbian/gay phonelines in North America are listed in the next chapter.
b) Get in touch with the next-nearest bi group to you. For example, if you're unable to reach the Washington Area Bisexual Support Group (in Maryland), call Bi-Ways in the D.C. area. Even if the next-nearest group is too far away for you to make it to regular meetings, perhaps members could help you in forming your own group or making further contacts.
c) Call one of the larger and more stable national or regional groups.

They are likely to have useful, up-to-date information, and are less likely to change their phone numbers than smaller groups. Try, for example, the one that serves the Boston networks, (617) 247-6683, the San Francisco number serving BiNET, USA: (415) 252-9818, or the Bisexual Phone Line serving Britain three nights weekly from 7:30 to 9:30 (81-569-7500 Tuesdays and Wednesdays, 31-557-3620 Thursdays). An invaluable resource is the *International Directory of Bisexual Groups* (see page 148).

3) At first, I had planned to list all groups that included "Bisexual" in their titles, such as the Oberlin Lesbian/Gay/Bisexual Union. But since more and more lesbian/gay groups are changing their names to accommodate bisexuals, I believe that most lesbian/gay groups will eventually do so and a change of name does not necessarily mean a change of attitude. One "lesbian/gay/bisexual" group that I know of, for example, barely tolerate bis, and only when they keep quiet about their heterosexuality; on the other hand, some "lesbian/gay" groups welcome as equals not only bisexuals but also transgenderists and other sexual minorities, and encourage all to exercise sexual self-determination.

Also not listed are "swingers" groups. Personally, I don't know enough about them to list them. From what I *do* know about them, I would be unable to say that they encourage one to exercise sexual self-determination in a noncoercive way.

4) I have listed only groups that have either a mailing address or phone number and that I have some reason to believe are active (e.g., listings in bi periodicals). I've tried to get additional information by correspondence, but have not always been successful.

5) Most groups do not like to give out the locations of their meeting places until after the person interested contacts them directly.

6) Sometimes people in rural areas would to be listed in bi periodicals as "contacts" for others in the same area. As this book is being marketed to a larger audience than those magazines, and is therefore more likely to be seen by biphobics, I chose not to list these people.

United States of America

National

BiNET, USA, P. O. Box 772, Washington, DC 20044, Tel: (415) 252-9818 (San Francisco)

This organization is meant to be a unifying body for the many and various bisexual organizations throughout the continent. Its goals include: alignment with such groups as the National Gay and Lesbian Task Force, creating a bibliography, arranging for representation at gay, lesbian, and straight conferences, and generally serving as a central source of resources for organizing, such as books, pamphlets, banners, buttons, and the like.

Once known as the North American Multicultural Bisexual Network, and before that as the National Bisexual Network, the organization began to come together around and during the Conference on Bisexuality held in San Francisco in June 1990. BiNET publishes a quarterly newsletter mentioned on page 147.

Bisexual Information and Counseling Service (BICS), 599 West End Avenue, Suite 1-A, New York, NY 10024, Tel: (212) 496-9500 (Staffed from 9 A.M. to 9 A.M. Eastern Time, Monday-Friday)

BICS is a nonprofit organization, funded by private donations, whose major goal is to provide information and educational counseling on health and relationship issues to self-identified bisexuals and their loved ones.

The professional staff consists of licensed health professionals whose function—in addition to staffing the free phone line—is to collect, evaluate, and disseminate information on health and relationship issues through the service's various service arms, after review and approval by a panel of consulting specialists.

In addition, BICS provides such services as:

- Publication of informational pamphlets on bisexual issues (provided free or at cost, depending on quantity);

- Distribution of pamphlets provided by related agencies, especially AIDS service agencies;
- One-on-one educational counseling on health and relationship issues (provided by appointment only);
- Maintenance of a "Community Resources List" of licensed health providers who desire to treat self-identified bisexuals and their loved ones. (Referrals will be made to interested persons without cost or obligations to either the provider or the patient);
- A listing of nonprofit organizations which specially welcome self-identified bisexuals and their loved ones, including religious, charitable, and support organizations; and
- For organizations, free on-site training programs of one to three hours in length on issues related to bisexuality.

BICS regularly reviews the latest research on health and relationship issues through its panel of consulting specialists. In the future, BICS hopes to be able to sponsor research as well.

Bi Amateur Publication Association, c/o Tom, 66 Franklin Street, Somerville, MA 02145

A place for bis to share writing, essays, poetry, comics, or whatever. The Bi Amateur Publication Association is similar to other APAs in the way that it works: members create their own magazines (of any size), make as many copies as there are members, and send them to the above address. The individual magazines received are then organized into packets which contain one copy of each magazine. These packets are then sent out to members.

The editors create and print the magazines and therefore have complete artistic control.

Fees may be required to cover postage, and editors will of course have to pay all production and printing costs. But for people interested in desktop publishing, the APA is a good way to get one's stuff seen by others with the same interests.

Regional

Bay Area Bisexual Network — *listed under* California

East Coast Bisexual Network, P.O. Box 639, Cambridge, MA 02140, Tel: (617) 247-6683 (617-BIS-MOVE or 617-BIS-NOTE)

The ECBN is a coalition of bisexual and bi-supportive individuals and groups in the Eastern U.S. Activities include an (approximately) annual conference and summer weekend retreat. ECBN may also serve as a source of seed money for new organizations and projects. Its steering committee is comprised of representatives of various areas on the East Coast from D.C. to Maine.

New York Area Bisexual Network — *listed under* New York

California

There are a number of groups in California of interest to bisexuals that are not listed here; either they are coalition groups which include bisexuals only incidentally, or they don't fit the criteria of this list in some other way.

For more information on groups in California, I strongly recommend the *Bisexual Resource Guide* which is published annually by the Bay Area Bisexual Network (see *Periodicals* listing). This 18-page booklet is available for $5.00, or is free with membership in BABN. In it are not only bi discussion groups (the main focus of this listing), but also AIDS resources, information services that regularly deal with information on bisexuality, and gay/lesbian-related groups.

Add Bis, 1234-1/8 N. Cahuenga Blvd., Hollywood, CA 90038, Tel: (213) 465-1053

A women-only group. Add Bis ("Advocates for Bisexuals") is a group that "encourages sexual diversity and welcomes anyone who is supportive of the bisexual movement." Specifically a *political-action* group, aimed at increasing awareness of bisexuality in the lesbian/gay community as well as in society in general. Also sponsors a support group.

Bay Area Bisexual Network, 2404 California Street #24, San Francisco, CA 94115, Tel: (415) 564-BABN(2226)

In addition to the usual rap groups, this network offers many other services, such as a bisexual speakers' bureau, as well as publishing a bimonthly newsletter.

Statement of Purpose

"The Bay Area Bisexual Network (BABN) is an alliance of bisexual and bi-supportive groups, individuals, and resources in the San Francisco Bay Area. BABN is coalescing the Bisexual community and creating a movement for acceptance and support of human diversity by coordinating forums, social events, opportunities, and resources.

"We support relationships among people regardless of gender, which can include relating intellectually, emotionally, spiritually, sensually, and sexually. We support celibacy, monogamy, and non-monogamy as equally valid lifestyle choices. We support open expression of affection and touch among people without such expression necessarily having sexual implications.

"BABN is by nature educational in that we are supporting the rights of all women and men to develop as whole beings without oppression because of age, race, religion, color, class, or different abilities, nor because of sexual preference, gender, gender preference and/or responsible consensual sexual behavior preferences. We also support acceptance in areas of employment, housing, healthcare, and education. This includes access to complete sexual information, free expression of responsible consensual sexual activity, and other individual freedoms.

"Membership is open to all bi-positive people whether or not they consider themselves bisexual."

Membership includes a subscription to the BABN *Newsletter* and a copy of the *Bisexual Resource Guide* and updates (see *Periodicals* listings), special mailings, and reduced-cost admission to BABN events.

BiForum, c/o Dr. Regina Reinhardt, 4305 Gesner Street, Suite 214, San Diego, CA 92117, Tel: (619) 259-8019

"We are a support group for bisexual individuals and couples. We meet once a month, every second Thursday, at 7 P.M.. Our meetings consist of two hours of sharing information and concerns and 30 minutes of socializing (with refreshments). Twice a year we meet socially for a potluck meal.

"Our membership consists of 70 people. We advertise in *The Reader* and all the gay papers to attract new members and offer them a safe and confidential environment to discuss their feelings.

"We have been in existence for six years (as of February, 1989). I have been the coordinator for the last four years and I am committed to keep the BiForum going as a needed community service."

The group was started in New York by Dr. Fritz Klein (author of *The Bisexual Option* and co-editor of the *Journal of Homosexuality*'s special issue on bisexuality: see articles in this volume), and was re-established in San Diego when he moved there in 1982.

BiFriendly San Francisco, 1406 Cole Street, San Francisco, CA 94117, Tel: Pierre (415) 753-0687 or Karla (415) 863-5961

An active social group of bisexual men and women who sponsor weekly socials/mixers and other events such as brunches, potlucks, camping outings, and dances for bisexuals and people friendly to bisexuals. Meets weekly at a restaurant in or near the Castro.

To receive monthly calendars outlining the group's future activities, send five legal-size, self-addressed stamped envelopes to the address above.

Note: In early 1990, other "BiFriendly" groups were starting up in the San Francisco area, including: BiFriendly of the South Peninsula which meets for dinner weekly (Contact: Steve, (415) 968-5902); BiFriendly of the East Bay, meeting for dinner twice monthly (Contact: Susan (male), (415) 524-2285); and BiFriendly of Santa Rosa (Contact Michael (707) 539-2569).

Bi-POL, 584 Castro Street Box #422, San Francisco, CA 94114, Tel: (415) 775-1190

Statement of Purpose

"BiPOL is an independent bisexual/lesbian/gay political organization, founded in 1983, which supports bisexual identity and rights. While BiPOL works in tandem with the more personal and social bi groups, it supports more militant public methods to *educate, advocate, and agitate* for bisexual visibility and inclusion. We believe in fighting to end the oppression of all people regardless of sexual or gender orientation, different abilities, race, age, culture, ethnicity, class, or religion.

"As an active and vital part of the lesbian and gay communities we believe in the fight to end the oppression of all sexual minorities will be assisted, not slowed, by the mass coming out of bisexuals in these communities.

"We strongly support sexual freedom: the freedom of all people, regardless of age, gender or different abilities, to explore and define openly their own sexual styles — bisexual, homosexual, heterosexual, self-sexual, celibate, monogamous, promiscuous, and nonmonogamous — with others who share the same freedom, responsibility, and consent. This includes the right to refuse sexual contact with anyone for any reason and the rights of women and men to take responsibility for and to control their own fertility.

"Our goals are to:
- Give bisexual orientation a strong, valid identity within the lesbian and gay liberation movement in particular, and society in general. In order to achieve this we must work as bisexuals within the movement both autonomously and collectively.

- Strive to assure that all those whose lives are affected by AIDS/HIV infection will receive compassionate, nonjudgmental respect, care, support, love, and assistance.
- Create a positive image of differing sexualities and sexual attitudes within the media. This necessitates representative and participatory control of the media. Also to create a media and culture of our own.
- Actively work for the self-organization of bisexual people and the coordination of existing bisexual groups, and to form alliances with other progressive forces nationally and internationally."

"Bis at The Center", The Center, 2017 East 4th Street, Long Beach, CA 90814 or P.O. Box 20917, Long Beach, CA 90801-3917. Tel: (213) 434-4455 or (213) 597-2799

"Bis at the Center" is an umbrella group for a number of bisexual-interest subgroups which meet at The [lesbian and gay] Center, the most central of which is the drop-in discussion/social meetings on Fridays from 8 to 10 P.M. At the time of this writing, the following subgroups are also being formed: a couples group (for heterosexual couples dealing with the emergence of one or both members' bisexuality); a men's group; a mixed group; a social group; a political group; and a questioning/coming out group.

In addition, the group has been working on creating new subgroups, such as a women's group and a young people's group. They are open to helping start other subgroups, if there is sufficient interest.

By Choice in L.A., c/o Joe, P.O. Box 3723, Granada Hills, CA 91334

A women's support group. Write for more information.

Pacific Center, 2712 Telegraph Ave., Berkeley, CA 94704, Tel: (415) 841-6224. MAILING ADDRESS: P.O. Box 908, Berkeley, CA 94701

Sponsors various sexuality groups, including a bisexual women's drop-in rap group which, at one time, also published a newsletter, *Bi-Lines.*

PanSocial Center, 7136 Matilija Ave., Van Nuys, CA 91405, Tel: (818) 989-3700 or (213) 873-3700

Also known as "The BiSocial Center," this group has expanded to cover all sexual orientations. Publishes a newsletter, *Panletter.*

Connecticut

Bi-Focal, c/o W.S.A., Wesleyan Station, Middletown, CT 06457

Bi-Focal is a confidential, informal rap/discussion group for bisexual and questioning women and men which meets weekly, and which works in conjunction with the university's G.L.B.A. (Gay, Lesbian, and Bisexual Alliance — "the political component of the gay community" at Wesleyan). In addition to the weekly meetings, Bi-Focal sponsors an annual workshop on bisexuality, usually in the spring.

The address listed above is permanent: however, to reach them more quickly, the following address will be in effect until May of 1991: Box 4152, Wesleyan University, Middletown, CT 06457

This group is most active during the school year (September-May).

Connecticut Network, 62 Arkay Drive, Higganum, CT 06441

This group was in formation in early 1990. Write for more information.

New Haven Bi Women's Support Group, P.O. Box 8192, New Haven, CT 06530

A women-only group. Write for more information.

District of Columbia
(Note: See also Maryland)

BiWays/Bisexuals of the Washington Area, P.O. Box 959, Washington, DC 20044

"We have been in existence since the early 1980s. We were originally known as Alpha/PM (plus/minus, i.e., both sides of the spectrum), but found [the name] to be [too] esoteric. We changed it in 1985 to BiWays. We used to meet weekly; now we do so monthly. We also sometimes meet socially."

This is a group for bisexual and bi-friendly people that welcomes diversity in both the membership and the content of the meetings, as the following quote from a 1989 newsletter shows:

"We have bis and bi-friendlies from all persuasions and walks of life, from straight-identified monogamous singles and marrieds to dyed-in-the-wool bisexual political activists (monogamous or not) to lesbian- and gay-identified celibates! We are proud of the open forum BiWays provides to the bisexual community in the D.C. area. People are welcome and encouraged to talk about whatever issues concern them at our functions; we are not a censorship group. There is too much censoring of others that already goes on in the world, and we do not wish to contribute to it in any way. BiWays will continue to put all possible effort into bringing more knowledge about and tolerance for bisexuals into our lives."

As for structure: "BiWays is not run by any one person. It is made up of, and decisions are made by, *all* of us. We do have a steering committee made up of representatives from both the men's and women's groups. All committee meetings are open to the group at large. Between the efforts of the steering committee and those of interested and active members (that means you!), we can be assured of a strong and influential Bi community in the D.C. area."

Bi-Ways is an affiliate of the East Coast Bisexual Network (see *Regional* listing).

BiWomen's and Men's Network, c/o BiWomen's Network, P.O. Box 2254, Washington, DC 20013-2254

The Washington, D.C. affiliate of the National Bisexual Network (see *National* listing).

Florida

Tampa Bay Bi-Ways (TBBW), P.O. Box 75163, Tampa, FL 33675

The first group to be started in Florida, TBBW was founded in August 1989 and is open to both men and women.

Illinois

Action Bi Women, 3225 N. Sheffield Avenue, Chicago, IL 60657, Tel: (312) 274-6956

A women-only group meeting at the Rodde Center, at the above address. According to the article "Chicago Bi-Ways: An Informal History" in *The Journal of Homosexuality*, Vol 11, #1/2, this group apparently grew out of the now-defunct group Chicago Bi-Ways.

Review, Box 7195, Westchester, IL 60153

This is a bi and gay men's group, although you wouldn't immediately pick that up from the group's literature. One of the founders of the group says, "Bi or gay isn't really the issue, because that fact won't change." It is run as a "monarchy", ". . . no officers, minutes of the last meeting, or committees. The agenda is determined by the men there."

The group has been in existence for over eight years, and current attendance averages about 10-20 men at each monthly meeting in Forest Park.

In addition to the monthly meetings, the following services are offered:

- Some sort of social event at least once every few months;
- An erotic book and magazine exchange; and
- A phone line 24 hours a day, 365 days a year.

They explicitly state that the group is *not* any of the following: a swinger's club, a dating service, a T.V. or transsexual group, an orgy group, or a therapy group. If you need any of the above, *Review is not for you*! But "... if you're looking for support and better understanding, along with a pleasant evening, give us a try."

Iowa

Bisexual Support Group, Gay Peoples' Union/Iowa Memorial Union, Iowa City, IA 52242

Maine

Maine Bisexual People's Network, P.O. Box 1792, Portland, ME 04104

"Currently [as of February, 1989], we are a diverse group of women and men ranging in age from sixteen to sixty-four. We are couples, singles, and friends. We are feminists, artists, parents, health-care workers, students, and teachers. We have created a safe, confidential community where anyone, regardless of sexual orientation, can explore and discuss issues related to bisexuality as well as have fun. We are committed to facilitating communication among bis and giving each other affirmative information and mutual support. Our group is not a place for therapy or for finding sexual partners.

"We sponsor picnics, potlucks, and other social activities on an irregular basis. This year, we hope to inaugurate a regular support group as well as to organize introductory meetings for new members. And we will continue to join other New England area bis in an annual bi winter retreat and cross-country ski weekend in Mid-coast Maine.

"Periodically, we publish a newsletter with information about local, regional, and national resources and events. Our confidential mailing list is used only to distribute this information to our members.

"If you would like to be on our mailing list and receive the newsletter and other information about upcoming events, please send a contribution of $5.00 or more (to cover costs) to the address shown above."

Statement of Purpose

"The purpose of the Maine Bisexual People's Network is to affirm in ourselves and others the positive nature of bisexuality and to work toward greater acceptance in the bisexual, gay, lesbian, and straight communities. We define bisexuality as the potential to feel emotionally and erotically attracted to both males and females.

"We accept and rejoice in our sexual orientation as well as those of others, seeing sexuality as a positive and integral part of physical, emotional, and spiritual health.

"We respect and nurture each other in making personal decisions about lifestyles and sexual expressions, believing in all persons' rights to explore, define, and redefine themselves as they choose.

"We see ourselves as pioneers in finding new ways to develop individual identities regardless of labels, creating fulfilling relationships, and challenging stereotypes within ourselves and others. We celebrate our diversity and seek ways to develop unity among the bisexual, gay, lesbian, and straight communities through education of ourselves and others.

"We see ourselves as part of the human-liberation movement and, as such, we support the liberation of all oppressed groups."

Maryland

Washington Area Bisexual Support Group, 8484 Annapolis Road #102, New Carrollton, MD 20784

This is a newly-formed group, intent on providing a space that is woman-friendly, while welcoming people of both sexes.

Massachusetts

BiCEP, c/o BBMN, P.O. Box 1645, Cambridge, MA 02238, Tel: (617) BIS-MOVE (247-6683)

BiCEP Statement of Aims
(Adopted September, 1988)

"The Bisexual Committee Engaging in Politics (BiCEP) is an organization whose aims include increasing awareness, visibility, and understanding of bisexual people, dispelling myths about and biased portrayals of bisexuals, supporting a wide range of lifestyle options, and working for full equality of all people. We oppose the emphasis on heterosexuality which gives special privilege to those with traditional lifestyles. We are committed to working for the acceptance of freely chosen, nonexploitative relationships and support nontraditional families, sexual preferences, and manners of loving. We recognize that all liberation movements are inherently linked, and we strive to confront injustice in all its forms, including oppression on the basis of sexual preference, gender, race, class, age, or disability.

"We recognize that we can maximize our accomplishments by working together with diverse groups of people that share our goals. We hope to achieve our aims by educating ourselves and society, as well as through political organizing and direct action. We advocate decentralized, grass-roots efforts as a means of achieving our objectives. We recognize the important contribution of all members of the group, and are thus organized as a collective, in order to meet the needs and express the views of each member."

Boston Bisexual Men's Network, Gay/Lesbian Services Center, 338 Newbury Street, Boston, MA 02115, Tel: (617) BIS-MOVE

The Boston Bisexual Men's Network (BBMN) is an organization which, like the Boston Bisexual Women's Network (see listing below), aims to provide a forum for people who are bisexual or interested in the subject of bisexuality. Although this group is specifically geared towards men, women are welcome to many of the functions, and projects are undertaken in cooperation with the women's network. The group publishes a newsletter, *BBMN News*.

Boston Bisexual Women's Network, Gay/Lesbian Services Center, 338 Newbury Street, Boston, MA 02115, Tel: (617) BIS-MOVE (Phone staffed 6 to 9 P.M. Mondays, answering machine at other times.)

With a mailing list of over 800, BBWN is a not-for-profit, collectively-run organization offering a bi-monthly newsletter, support groups, social events, a speaker's bureau, weekly rap group, introductory meetings, and archives.

BBWN is open to all women regardless of current sexual identity or ability to pay. Membership, which includes a subscription to *Bi Women* (the newsletter), is $16/year (or on a sliding scale, based on ability to pay). See also the *Periodicals* listing and the interview with Robyn Ochs, "Where the Boys Aren't" elsewhere in this volume.

Valley Bisexual Network, 24 Cowles Road, Amherst, MA, 01002

According to its founders, The Valley Bisexual Network was started in March 1987, with a gathering of about 25 people. From this, the group grew and gained confidence while maintaining the decision to stay low-key, have fun, and provide a space for casual gatherings. By the following spring, the group had a mailing list of over 100 people, who were notified of special events, such as potlucks, a dance party, and a bisexual contingent to march in Gay Pride parades in Boston and Northampton.

The rap group, which now meets about every other week at the University of Massachusetts, was started in the spring of 1988. The makeup of the group varies from meeting to meeting, with about ten "core" members.

Michigan

Bi Support Group, P.O. Box 1621, Royal Oak, MI 48068

Minnesota

The Bisexual Connection, P.O. Box 13158, Minneapolis, MN 55414

Founded in November 1985, this group meets once a month for an open discussion and potluck dinner, as well as having special planning meetings to organize projects and activities.

The group exists to provide a "safe, positive, nonsexist, and open environment" where bisexually-identified people can celebrate themselves and each other, share from their own experience, share information, and discuss issues and explore interests in common. It is open to all people, no matter what their culture, marital/relationship status, affectional sexual preference, or age (as long as it's over 18). It "is not intended to be a substitute for a therapy group nor is it a social club."

Publishes a quarterly newsletter, the *Bifocal*. (Donation appreciated.) Also, is currently compiling a "nationwide list of bi-friendly services available to bisexual people, including businesses such as bars and retailers as well as clubs and so forth."

The Bisexual Connection is registered with the State of Minnesota as a nonprofit organization.

Bisexual Pride, c/o The Bisexual Connection, P.O. Box 13158, Minneapolis, MN 55414

Bisexual Pride is the political arm of the above-mentioned group. It focuses on "the political implications of bisexuality and on community education relating to bisexuality."

Missouri

S.L.B.W.S.G., c/o J. Seelig, 7239 Tulane, Apt. #1 West, St. Louis, MO 63130

A women-only group.

New Mexico

Bisexual Women's Group: contact through the Lesbian Helpline, Tel: (505) 255-7288.

"I am trying to start a support group for bisexual women in the Albequerque area . . . There are just beginning to be enough of us that we will start meeting soon.

"I believe that we will be talking about the internal confusions and external isolations of being bisexual. Being a strong feminist myself, I will try to make that perspective part of the framework. I also hope for political action to evolve from it: i.e., a bisexual contingent in the Gay Pride march here."

New York

New York Area Bisexual Network (NYABN), P.O. Box 497, Times Square Station, New York, NY 10108

A cooperative consisting of the following resources:

Bisexual Pride

A place for bisexual men and women to meet and explore community and personal issues in an informal, friendly setting. Meets Sundays, 3 P.M. at the Lesbian/Gay Community Services Center, 208 West 13th Street.

Bi-Ways New York

An recently formed organization which plans cultural and recreational activities: beach parties, picnics, theater, etc. Meets at least one Saturday per month. Call or write for more information.

BIDSS (Bisexual Dominance and Submission Support Group)

Provides a "no-pressure" setting for discussion of issues pertaining to consensual power exchange between bisexuals. Meets the first Sunday of each month at 4:45 P.M. at the Lesbian/Gay Community Services Center, 208 West 13th Street.

BiPAC (Bisexual Political Action Committee)

BiYouth

New youth group.

New York City Bisexual Support Group, P.O. Box 2550, Manhattanville Station, New York, NY 10027

Meets the second Sunday of each month at New York City's Lesbian/Gay Community Services Center (208 West 13th Street). This group was founded in 1980 by Bill Himelhoch, who single-handedly administered it until December 1988, when he moved to Boston. A statement from Mr. Himelhoch:

"The Bisexual Support Group brings together women and men

who want to affirm the bisexuality in human experience. In a metropolis such as New York City, which tolerates and encourages limitless diversity, we face a special challenge. The many people who feel troubled, outcast, or misunderstood because of their bisexual attractions have radically different life experiences. Some have primary loyalties to the gay cultures, others to the straight cultures; their understanding of gender roles, their sexual preferences and their ways of life may be worlds apart.

"This extraordinary diversity sometimes presents an obstacle to maintaining a safe, nonjudgmental meeting place where every person's story is accepted. A special effort is necessary to listen to every story no matter how much it is at variance to our own and to state our point of view or share feelings without attacking or condemning others.

"The group has maintained a firm commitment to the principle of unconditional acceptance. We want to create a group safe for every person to speak about difficult, tender feelings not shared in other places; a group that not only tolerates diverse views and activities but enables each person to feel confirmed and uplifted."

Rochester Bisexual Men's Network ATTN: Jack, c/o The Empty Closet, 713 Monroe Ave., Box F, Rochester, NY 14607

Rochester Bisexual Women's Network, c/o Michelle, P.O. Box 24804, Rochester, NY 14624

Formed in April 1988, the RBWN meets one Sunday a month and offers potlucks, socializing, support, and more. Meetings are held at members' homes.

Womyn's Bi Pride & Support Group, 79 Central Avenue, Albany, NY 12210

Meets monthly.

Ohio

Bi Group, 3387 W. 86th Street, Cleveland, OH 44102

Bi-Lines, P.O. Box 14773, Columbus, OH 43214

The group meets the 2nd and 4th Thursdays of each month for discussion, and plans are underway to increase the frequency of other social events such as "gallery hops" (evenings spent going from art gallery to art gallery in Columbus' Short North District).

Because members have had difficulties in the past with harassment, they now require that you write to them at the above address, mentioning your reasons for wanting to take part in the group, and they will get back to you with an address for the next meeting. They ask that you contribute towards rental of the room and group expenses.

[I've been to several meetings of this group, and can recommend it as an oasis in the otherwise barren Midwest. Typically there are about five to eight people at each meeting, and new members are frequent. The discussion is free-form, and often centers around subjects that are relevant to members' lives at the time. While women outnumber men, there is usually at least one male at each meeting. — T.G.]

There are no officers, elections, or committees. This is a discussion group first and foremost, typically run pretty much by one person with assistance from other members.

Bi Women's Support Group, P.O. Box 594, Northfield, OH 44067

Oregon

Portland Bisexual Forum, P.O. Box 1141, Portland, OR 97211

Meets biweekly.

The Questioning Circle (QC) and Alternate Sexualities Integrated at Swarthmore (AsIs), Swarthmore College, Swarthmore, PA 19081

The Questioning Circle is a discussion group for people interested in exploring issues of concern to people who are questioning their sexual orientation, and it meets in private once a week (location posted on the AsIs bulletin board). These meetings are usually attended by five to eight people. AsIs is a student group for all people lesbian, gay, or bi, with the purpose of bettering conditions for sexual minorities at Swarthmore.

History of the groups: the Questioning Circle (QC) is the latest incarnation of the Bisexual and Questioning Circle (BQC), which started as an outgrowth of the Gay and Lesbian Union (GLU) at Swarthmore College. It was started to create a place for people who were unsure of their sexual orientation, unsure of their sexual feelings, or coming out as a sexual minority. The group gained notoriety on campus as being more discussion-oriented and less "political" than its companion sexual-minority group.

But because, as Ellie Weiss '90 put it, "you don't have to be bi to have questions about your sexual orientation and you don't have to be uncertain to be bi," the group dropped the "Bisexual" from their name and decided to call themselves the "Questioning Circle," welcoming all people interested in discussing sexuality in general, and minority sexuality in particular.

For bisexuals, lesbians, and gays at Swarthmore who are more "out" and certain of their sexual identities, there is now the group AsIs, which has taken the place of the old Gay and Lesbian Union. This group has a focus which is "political, with some attention to social pleasures."

Activities for the Questioning Circle are now largely administered through AsIs, which has an office on the third floor of the student center, Tarble-in-Clothier. The office, though not regularly staffed, maintains a library of books and resources of interest to gay, lesbian, and bisexual people. AsIs also has a paid student intern to oversee activities in the group; unfortunately, this contact person changes from year to year.

South Carolina

Lowcountry Alternative Lifestyles, 1408 Lieben Road, Mount Pleasant, SC 29464

Formerly known as "Counseling for Alternative Lifestyles."

Washington (state)

Bisexual Support Group (Address: BSG, P.O. Box 7231, Seattle, WA 98133)

A coed group, with activities twice a month.

Seattle Bisexual Men's Network, c/o Seattle Bisexual Women's Network (see below)

Seattle Bisexual Women's Network, P.O. Box 30645, Greenwood Station, Seattle, WA, 98103-0645, Tel: (206) 783-7987

This group meets regularly and puts out a newsletter, *North Bi Northwest* (see separate listing, *Periodicals*). In addition, it was recently accepted as a member of Seattle's Gay Community Social Services group; as a result, it has tax-exempt, nonprofit status.

Statement of Purpose:
"We are a group of feminists working for full equality for bisexual people in both the heterosexual and lesbian/gay communities.

"We regard ourselves as part of the larger sexual minority community, and consider the fight for lesbian/gay liberation to be our own.

"We are dedicated to the right of all people to define their own sexuality, free from any social, political, or economic coercion.

"We seek to provide a safe place for women to explore all aspects of their sexuality.

"All women are welcome to attend all SBWN activities. While we work cooperatively with men on issues of common interest, our group is exclusively female to keep the concerns of women always in the forefront of our work.

"The discrimination we face, as women and as sexual minorities, is only one facet of oppression; all bigotry is our enemy.

"We stand behind the racial and ethnic liberation movements and the struggle for economic equality. In any work we do, feminism and the interests of bisexuals will always be our central concern."

Goals:

- Provision of emotional and social support for all women exploring bisexual issues.
- Universal acceptance of the integrity of bisexuality, within both the lesbian/bi/gay and heterosexual communities.
- Positive social, legal, and political acknowledgement of bisexuality.
- Discussion and education about bisexuality and specific bisexual issues within our community and in society.
- Cooperation with other bisexual and bi-supportive groups nationally and worldwide.

INTERNATIONAL

CANADA

British Columbia

Bi-Focus, P.O. Box 34172, Post Office D, Vancouver BC, V6J 4N1, Canada

This is a confidential support group which meets every other week ("bi-weekly"), most often in members' living rooms. Its goal is first and foremost to provide a supportive, alcohol and drug-free environment for bisexual people, as well as providing education and opportunities for "social networking." But note: the group is not a "pick-up" club; social activities are secondary to the primary functions of support and education.

A gender-mixed group, Bi-Focus has found it necessary to "screen" people who want to become active in the group. If, after a few meetings, it becomes apparent that the new member is only there to look for sex, he (or, theoretically, she) will be asked to leave.

The group maintains ties with nearby bi groups, including the Seattle Bisexual Women's Network and the Bi Community Forum in Portland, Oregon. It also produces a quarterly newsletter, *Bi-Line*; see *Periodicals* listing for more information.

Statement of Purpose

"Bi-Focus is a Vancouver-based support group which meets weekly in order to provide a safe place for women and men to discuss their bisexuality.

"We are dedicated to the right of all people to define their own sexuality free from any social, political, or economic coercion.

"Bi-Focus is involved nationally with other individuals and organizations which are active in the struggle against oppression caused by sexism, racism, or lifestyle. We seek to bring about acceptance and equal rights in areas of employment, housing, medical care, economic equality, individual freedom, sexual education, and free expression of all mutually consenting sexual activity."

Bi-Focus Goals

- To provide emotional and social support for women and men exploring bisexual issues.
- Universal acceptance of the integrity of bisexuality within lesbian/bi/gay and heterosexual communities.
- Discussion and education about bisexuality and bisexual issues within our communities and in society.
- To create a mutually caring, open community based on the practice of nonjudgmental listening, sharing, and growing.

Vancouver Bi Group, Box 3287, Vancouver, BC V6B 3X9, Canada

Manitoba

Yourself, P.O Box 2790, Winnipeg, Manitoba R3C 3R5, Canada

Ontario

Ontario Bisexual Network, Box 95, Station O, 912 O'Connor Drive, Toronto, Ontario M4A 2M8, Canada

Québec

Les Capables Bisexual Group, c/o Marcus, Box 966, Station H, Montréal, Québec H3G 2M9, Canada

GREAT BRITAIN

Bisexual Phoneline: 031-557-3620, Thursdays, 7:30 — 9:30 P.M. (Located in Edinburgh, Scotland; serves all of Great Britain)

ENGLAND

East Anglia

University of East Anglia Bisexual Group, University House, UEA, Norwich, Norfolk

Welcomes nonstudents.

London Area

Bisexual Artists/Performers/Writers/Musicians Network, c/o London Bisexual Group (see below)

"Some performers are starting to work together in London, and we'd like to get people together from all over to make pieces for events like the national conference."

London Bisexual Group (Address: LBG, BM BI, London WC1N 3XX, England)

Meets every Friday.

The London Bisexual Group is perhaps the largest and most active of the bi groups in Europe, publishing *Bi-Monthly: The Magazine for Bisexuals* (see *Periodicals* listing) and organizing the annual National Bi Conference for Great Britain.

The group was founded in September 1981, and an extensive constitution has been drawn up to formalize the structure of the organization and ensure its continuing success. The executive board has ten members, equally divided as to gender: a chair, vice-chair, secretary, treasurer, and six committee members. At the time of this writing, two of the board members are nonbisexual "allies."

The London Bisexual Group "is open to people of all sexual identities, and aims to provide a relaxed but stimulating atmosphere."

London Bisexual Women's Group, BM LBWG, London WC1N 3XX, England

"The London Bisexual Women's Group is an open group for women of all ages. We meet monthly in each other's homes for discussion, support, and fun. All women are welcome to join us."

Radical Black Bisexual Caucus, BM 4390, London WC1N 3XX

Manchester Area

Manchester Men's Bisexual Group, P.O. Box 153, Manchester M60 1LP, England, Tel: 061-274-3999 (The Manchester Gay Centre, answered daily, 4 - 10 P.M.).

A social group of Bisexual Men/Women who meet at the Manchester Gay Centre on Sidney Street, around the corner from the Eighth Day Cafe, on the first Thursday of every month. A support, discussion, and social group, similar to the Manchester Women's Bisexual Group (below).

Manchester Women's Bisexual Group (Address: WBG, P.O. Box 153, Manchester M60 1LP, England), Tel: 061-274-3999 (The Manchester Gay Centre, answered daily, 4 - 10 P.M.).

Started in June 1987, this women-only group now meets the second Thursday of every month at the Manchester Gay Centre (see address in preceding listing). The group is a support, discussion, and social group which usually draws between 10 and 20 women to the meetings, after which some of them will often go to one of the gay pubs, or to a gay/feminist play or film if one is showing nearby.

Wiltshire

Wessex Bisexual Group, c/o K. Peck, c/o LBG, BM BI, London WC1N 3XX, England

Meets irregularly at a venue in Wiltshire.

Yorkshire

Hull University Bisexual Group, Union Building, Cottingham Road, Hull, East Yorkshire, England

Meets weekly during school times in the university's Union Building.

Leeds Bisexual Group, 98, Bankside Street, Leeds 8, England

Meets fortnightly at the Leeds Peace Centre as well as having social events at irregular intervals.

York Bisexual Group (Address: YBG, P.O. Box 284, York YO1 1TX, England)

Meets the 2nd Monday of each month.

Other England

At the time of writing, groups were forming in Birmingham, Bristol, Newcastle, and Tyneside. Phone 031-557-3620 on Thursdays from 7:30 to 9:30 P.M. for more information.

SCOTLAND

Edinburgh

Edinburgh Bisexual Group, c/o Lesbian and Gay Community Centre, 58A Broughton, Edinburgh, Scotland, or call Bisexual Phoneline, 031-557-3620

The Edinburgh group is one of the more active in Britain, maintaining the Bisexual Phoneline (listed above), publishing and sending out a monthly newsletter to a mailing list of over 100, running a pen-pal scheme, and holding weekly meetings, which are usually attended by between six and twenty people. They meet every Thursday night in the Lesbian and Gay Centre, as follows: first Thursday: newcomers night; second Thursday: discussions on pre-arranged topics (coming out, loneliness, etc).; third Thursday: social night ("When we bring drink and music and have a chat."); and fourth Thursday: discussion night (like second Thursday).

After the Thursday meetings, some of the members of the group usually go out to a local pub for a drink. In addition to the Thursday meetings, they also arrange social events such as picnics, theater trips, walks, swimming, meals, etc.

There is no formal "leadership" within the group. "Basically, regular attenders take on certain jobs."

The group maintains contacts with other bisexual groups in

Great Britain and around the world, and takes part in the annual British national conference.

Other Scotland

At the time of this writing, groups are also forming in Ayr and Glasgow. Call the Bisexual Phoneline (031-557-3620, Thursdays, 7:30 to 9:30 P.M.) for more information.

THE NETHERLANDS

(From the Boston Bisexual Men's Network's *Bi-Monthly* [now *BBMN News*], December 1987): "I have just returned from Amsterdam, which is the best city on earth for bi travellers. Places actually advertise that they cater to gays *and* bisexuals! There are great museum, good bars, flavored condoms (strawberry, lime, licorice, and, of course, banana).... What more could a person want? O.K., you do have to know how to politely turn down a business deal with a 14-year-old, but it's still a very interesting city." — Wayne.

Landelijk Netwerk Bisexualiteit, Postbus 5087, 1007 AB Amsterdam, The Netherlands Tel: Vroomshoop 05498-44384

"The Dutch national bisexual network started in 1983 as the Landelijke Steun-en Aktiergroep Biseksualiteit (National Bisexual Support and Action Group). They organized a country-wide bi-day, which was attended by about 350 people. In several parts of the country, bi groups were begun." A continuing organization: call or write for more information.

Werkgroep Bi Nijmegen, c/o Fred, Zellersacker 15-49, 6546 HL, Nijmegen, The Netherlands

Werkgroep Bisexualiteit Amsterdam, p/a Rozenstraat 14, 1016 NX Amsterdam, The Netherlands. Tel: 020-254671 (Selmar), 020-277445 (Wouter)

"Our group wants bisexuals to meet each other; we organize an evening each month: sometimes a movie, a lecture or a debate, sometimes a disco-evening. We also bring people together if they want to talk with other bisexuals. Furthermore, there is a weekly local radio program on a cable radio station in Amsterdam. The group itself meets every three weeks to get things organized."

Werkgroep Biseksualiteit c/o NVSH-afd. Haarlem, Ripperdastraak 11, 2011 KG Haarlem, The Netherlands, Tel: 023-326602

NEW ZEALAND

Wellington Bisexual Women's Group, c/o Diana Suggate, 90 Elizabeth Street, Mount Victoria, Wellington, New Zealand

Meets fortnightly (bi-weekly) for a shared meal, discussion, and support. This, the first known group in the Southern Hemisphere, has recently started out with a handful of committed members. As one organizer wrote, "We may sound small, but there are only about 200,000 people in Wellington and 3 million in the whole country!"

WEST GERMANY

Initiative Bisexualler Frauen & Manner, c/o "Die Lade", 'Bi-Initiative', Karl-Marx-Strasse 58, D1000 Berlin 44, West Germany Tel: 030/62437 61 (Thursdays, 11 A.M. — 1 P.M.)

This is an organized, nationwide West German group of bisexual women and men which has met continuously since 1984. Until 1987, these meetings were open to everybody, but during 1988 the group felt a need to work on its own processes and organization, and so it met as a closed group and eschewed more "public" activities.

Now the group is turning outwards once again, and welcomes interested people to get involved. They kicked off their grand re-opening with a "Bisexuality Workshop," open to the public, which was held on the weekend of March 31-April 4, 1989. The regular meetings are held on weekends four times a year at different places in Germany and feature "self-counseling, biography-talks and discussions of issues concerning lesbian, gay, or bisexual lifestyles or sexual identities." as well as "feasts, dancing, and laughing."

OTHER RESOURCES

Computer

> Utopian Network, P.O. Box 1146, New York, NY 10156. Two numbers, up to 2400 bauds: (516) 842-7518 (24 hours) and (212) 686-5248 (8 P.M. - noon; voice all other times)
> • Sysops: Gillian Boardman (212 number) and Adam Selene (516 number)

These two numbers lead to computer bulletin-board services (BBS's) for people interested in "alternate lifestyles" (bisexuals, transgenderists, swingers, lesbians/gays, etc.). Both of the boards share the same database and are accessed with the payment of one membership, but the (516) number has a slightly less stringent security system, allowing users more access.

Access at the lowest level ("stranger") is free, but does not allow the user to do much: it is mostly used as an introduction to the system. A "basic" membership ($15/year) allows a greater degree of access (permission to read messages, post, etc.), and a "regular" membership ($25/year) allows even more. There is also a "full" membership available, which opens the system up to the greatest degree available to the user. This level cannot be bought; it is earned through regular participation in discussions, helpfulness, and honesty. The granting of "full" membership status is done only through the judgment of the sysops.

The Utopian Network is also a clearing house for information about other "alternative-lifestyle"-interest BBS's throughout the United States. At the time of this writing, people connected with the Utopian Network are compiling a directory of such BBS's: call, write, or dial in for more information.

Mail.alternates, VAX: alternates.dadla.la.tek.com (On BITNET).
• **Sysop: Hank Buurman.**

"Mail.alternates is an E-mail group of people who advocate and/or practice open sexual lifestyles. Its members are primarily bisexual men and women and their significant others. Mail.alternates is intended as a forum and support group for adult men and women who espouse freedom of choice and imagination in human sexual relations. Those who are offended by frank and uninhibited discussions relating to sexual issues should not subscribe."

Mail.alternates is run as a mailing-list service: send a message to the address above and it will be forwarded to all members of the mailing list; in this way, everybody's anonymity is guaranteed. It is requested that your first message be a short biography, which can be as personal and revealing as you like. If you feel uncomfortable about divulging your true identity (or if you are protective of your privacy), feel free to use a pseudonym; in fact, most members do.

Because of the special medium of computer communication, which often encourages people to be more personal, Mail.alternates has become one of the freest, most open, and most respectful forums for discussing sexuality that I've ever seen. People of all sexual preferences and "perversions" talk openly about themselves, and counter-discussions are always polite and nonthreatening. Erotica is welcome, as are items that do not directly involve sexuality (news, advice, etc.).

Unfortunately the group, like soc.motss (listed above), is only available through mainframe computer, to which few people have access. The best place to look for access is your local college or university which may offer mainframe access to students free of charge and may rent (or give) time to outsiders on a case-by-case basis.

San Francisco AIDS Foundation (support groups for heterosexual and bisexual men and their female partners), attention: Christopher Alexander, P.O. Box 6182, San Francisco, CA 94101-6182, Tel: (415) 864-5855 ext. 2511

"The SF AIDS Foundation provides comprehensive social services for men and women with AIDS or ARC. Information on and assistance with accessing the following is available: medical services, counseling, insurance, disability benefits, home care, updated AIDS information, etc.

"Of particular interest to bisexual men is a support group that meets weekly for heterosexual and bisexual men with HIV infection or an AIDS or ARC diagnosis. The group is free, is drop-in, and once a month meets with the women's AIDS/ARC group that we sponsor."

(A point of trivia: The Honorary Board of Directors includes actors Whoopi Goldberg and Richard Gere.)

Defunct Organizations of Note

Arete, Whittier, CA

According to the October, 1988 issue of *Bisexuality: News, Views, and Networking*: "This was a very large social/support/sexual group in Los Angeles that appears to have disbanded due to AIDS, etc., but its founder, Marvin Colter, now runs Hands and Hearts for Men."

Chicago Bi-Ways, Chicago, IL

Was apparently an active group for quite a few years, as is described in the article "Chicago Bi-Ways: An Informal History" in *Journal of Homosexuality,* Vol 11 #1/2, but has disappeared since the publication of that article.

The Bulletin Board, New York, NY

Published broadsides of news and features of interest to bisexuals.

MALIS Alliance, Philadelphia, PA

A former member of this organization called on October 11, 1988 to tell me that the group is no longer in existence, after 30 years of productive activity, making this probably the oldest "sexual alternates" group in America (besides those strictly concerned with homosexuality). All information below is based on that one phone call, and has not been verified by any other source.

Founded on June 27, 1958, it was originally an underground organization unifying people of many different "alternate" sexual lives (including cross-dressers, bisexuals, homosexuals, etc.). The name, in fact, is an acronym for "Many Associations Listed In Secrecy" — apparently, anti-"obscenity" laws of the time prohibited meetings of such people, using the excuse that they would be harmful to society. In 1972, the group became legal, and was able to advertise itself.

The group sustained itself and grew despite (or perhaps, because of) such laws, and at its height it had a "staff" of 25 people and hundreds of members. It reached out to become an international group, and maintained connections with people and groups in London, New York, The Netherlands, Germany, Australia, and Hong Kong, among others. It also sponsored projects such as the Bisexual Female International Hotline and The International Project.

As other groups sprang up to deal more specifically with the various minorities, MALIS eventually became mainly a bisexual group. In the 70s, it encounted some bi-phobic bigotry in trying to reach out. The London Gay Switchboard refused to list them as a referral, for example, and the German gay paper *Der Ich* refused to print their ads. But when *The London Gay News* eventually did accept their ads, the result was over 800 responses between 1979 and 1981.

The group began to die in 1982 when divisiveness and apathy began to thin its ranks. Lesbians and bisexual women were finding the group to be unfriendly to them, so they tended to join either exclusively female groups or more female-friendly groups. And, as a result, some men turned away from such an exclusively male group. With the decrease in both human and financial resources, the organization closed in February 1988.

Radical Lesbian and Gay Identified Bisexual Network, Brighton, England

The Bisexual Center, San Francisco, CA

At one time this was *the* center for bisexual activity on the West Coast; the gap caused by its passing has been admirably filled by other San Francisco organizations, most notably the Bay Area Bisexual Network and Bi-POL (See *California* listings.)

The Seattle Bisexual Support Network, Seattle, WA

The network published a newsletter, *Bi and Large*, as well as having meetings. Last seen in 1987. Its passing has been filled by the Seattle Bisexual Women's Network (see *Washington* listing — for women only).

mom ... dad ... I'm bicoastal.

Graphic: Ursula H. Roma
© 1987 Cincinnati, Ohio

A Note on Lesbian and Gay Phonelines

The gay/lesbian movement has much more support than does the bi movement, and bi resources are still too few and far between. In many cases, however, the support systems designed for lesbians and gays are of use to bis: after all, much of the difficulty in being bi comes from reconciling homosexual feelings in a society that demands compulsory heterosexuality. While it is true that some gay-centered organizations are hostile to bis, this is changing, and most gay and lesbian phonelines are able to help callers regardless of their sexual preferences/orientations.

I think it's important that bisexuals keep in touch with lesbian/gay communities, for two reasons: because it's easy to lose one's feelings of pride and self-worth without the support that they can offer; and they, in turn, deserve our support. For without the continuation of a strong gay/lesbian community, bisexual rights and communities will quickly die.

For a nearly complete listing of those phonelines, I strongly recommend *The Gayellow Pages* (Renaissance House: Box 292, Village Station, New York, NY 10014). This book is updated annually, and offers tens of thousands of resource listings (addresses, phone numbers, and comments) for lesbian/gay and lesbian/gay-friendly people.

Without such a directory, one would do well to look in the local phone book for "gay" and "lesbian" numbers (sometimes preceded by the name of the community). If you find nothing there, phone the National Gay and Lesbian Hotline at (800) 767-4297 and ask for a local gay and/or lesbian referral.

Local phone numbers are usually only tended to a few hours each week; if you can't get through at first, keep trying. Best times to try: evenings between 6 and 10 P.M.

—T.G.

Periodicals on Bisexuality

Note: This book's Directory of Bisexual Special-Interest Groups lists many organizations that publish newsletters, and I have not attempted to include them all here. I have tried to include periodicals that go beyond the basic newsletter format to publish articles of more than local interest. I apologize if I have missed some publications that deserved to be listed. Readers and staff members should send me samples of any publication they think should be listed in care of Times Change Press, P. O. Box 1380, Ojai, CA 93024, and I'll try to include them in later editions of this book. Several addresses and phone numbers — but not necessarily any other material — have been substantially updated for the third printing, and some new titles have been added, with the help of Robyn Ochs, the friendly and capable editor of the *International Directory of Bisexual Groups* (see below), of whose efforts Times Change Press and I are most appreciative. — T. G.

Anything That Moves: Beyond the Myths of Bisexuality, c/o BABN, 2404 California Street #24, San Francisco, CA 94115, Tel: (415) 564-BABN
   A very good and large new quarterly, with feature articles and regular sections on "health and growth" and "arts and culture," including reviews, fiction, and poetry of more than local interest. Only the resources and calendar sections are limited to the Bay Area. Subscriptions, which include membership in the Bay Area Bisexual Network, have initially been set at $25 per year (limited income $16, foreign and groups/institutions $30). Additional contributions and advertisements are always welcome. A sample issue costs $6.
   The mailing list is kept strictly confidential and mailings are discreet.

BiFOCUS, P. O. Box 30372, Philadelphia, PA 19103
   A bimonthly newsletter for men and women in the Philadelphia area. Annual subscriptions are $12, with a low-income rate of $4 and an institutional or supporting rate of $20.

Bifrost: A National Monthly Newsletter for Bisexuals, P. O. Box 117, Norwich NR1 2SU, England.

Currently a two-page newsletter with resource listings, news, poetry, and articles. A year's sub costs £6.5 (waged) or £3 (unwaged).

Bi-Issues, 50 Ash Grove, London N13 5AR, England.

Published from four to six times a year, this journal of opinion is aimed primarily at a British audience and priced, presumably per issue, at £1.50 (waged) or four first-class stamps (unwaged).

Bi-Line, c/o Bi-Focus, P. O. Box 34172, Post Office D, Vancouver BC V6J 4N1, Canada, Tel: (604) 737-0513

At last report this quarterly newsletter was free of charge. However, a by-mail subscriber should, whenever possible, make a donation to the group to cover postage and printing costs. Contributions of articles, fiction, letters, etc. are welcome.

BiNet, USA, P. O. Box 772, Washington, DC 20044-0772

The newly-named successor group to the North American Multicultural Bisexual Network plans to publish a quarterly four-page bulletin. It will have regular columns, including tips for organizers, news and events of national interest, and lists of resource materials. Information on subscribing can be obtained from the above address or by phoning the San Francisco office, 415-252-9818.

Bi-Us, P. O. Box 1912, London N16 5AU, England

This magazine costs £5 for four issues, with checks made payable to Melting Pot Publishers.

Bi Women, c/o BBWN, Box 639 Cambridge, MA 02140, Tel: (617) BIS-MOVE (247-6683)

This is one of the best periodicals available, well written and cleverly laid out. Subscriptions to this 12-to-16-page bimonthly are open to both men and women, although it remains a "women's space," with editorial decisions to be made by women only. The basic subscription rate is $18 per year, with a sliding scale downward and upward.

The mailing list is kept strictly confidential and never given or sold outside of the Boston Bisexual Women's Network. Newsletters are mailed in discreet security envelopes.

BBMN News, c/o BBMN, 95 Berkeley Street #613, Boston, MA 02115, Tel: (617) BIS-MOVE (247-6683)

Although this is the newsletter for the Boston Bisexual Men's Network, subscriptions to this monthly magazine are open to everybody. At the time of this writing, the cost is $12/year, payable to BBMN.

International Directory of Bisexual Groups, c/o East Coast Bisexual Network, P. O. Box 639, Cambridge, MA 02140, Tel: (617) BIS-MOVE (247-6683)

This guide, compiled by ECBN member Robyn Ochs, is continually updated, and published every April and October. Cost is $5 per copy.

North Bi Northwest, c/o Seattle Bisexual Women's Network, P. O. Box 30645, Greenwood Station, Seattle, WA 98103-0645, Tel: (206) 783-7987

The newsletter of the Seattle Bisexual Women's Network, especially relevant to people living in that area of the continent. (Often has contributions from the other two nearby bi groups, in Portland, Oregon and Vancouver, British Columbia.) The subscription rate is: $15/year (regular) and $10/year (low income). Published bimonthly.

Polyfidelitous Educational Productions, P.O. Box 5247, Eugene, OR 97405

Although not specifically bisexual, this organization specializes in producing materials about the "polyfidelitous" way of life, which, by definition, includes bisensuality.

This definition of "polyfidelity" is by the editor of *Peptalk* — from its Summer (July), 1988 issue:

"Polyfidelity is a sexually fidelitous marriage of more than two adults in which all partners are valued equally (no primaries or secondaries). The word originated with the Keristan Commune in the early seventies in an attempt to create a word to describe the lifestyle they were living. 'Poly,' of course, indicates multiplicity and 'fidelity' refers to loyalty and conjugal fidelity (sexual exclusivity) to the group."

P.E.P. produces the following publications:

• *Primer* ("essentials of the lifestyle"), $2.00;

• "Profile" ("questionnaire to clarify values"), $2.00; and

• *Peptalk* (quarterly newsletter), offered with membership — see below.

It also sells an audio tape ("lifestyle discussion on cassette") for $3.50 and a PEP T-shirt (100% cotton: M, L, XL) for $10.00.

Membership is in three categories: "audience" (receives quarterly newsletter), $9.00; supporting member (receives *Primer*, "Profile," newsletter, and access to member network), $18.00; and full member (receives the same three publications, and free access to membership network. Also receives complimentary copies of all publications and free admission to all activities), $60.00.

A Bibliography on Bisexuality
by Charles Steir (before 1984) and Thomas Geller (1984 and later)

From *The Journal of Homosexuality*, Spring 1985 ("Bisexualities: Theories and Research," 11(1/2), edited by Fritz Klein and Timothy Wolf). Used with permission, with additions by Mr. Steir and Mr. Geller.

Mr. Steir points out that, even though it is the most exhaustive bibliography on bisexuality and related issues (such as androgyny) to date, it is not perfect. There is other information, not listed here, in such sources as anthropological and biological texts; film, theatre, and fiction; autobiographies; gay and lesbian publications; newspapers columns; pornographic and erotic publications; and finally, foreign sources of all of the above, present and past. He hopes to bring out a more complete listing in the future.

Aaron, W. [pseud.] 1972. *Straight: A heterosexual talks about his homosexual past.* New York: Doubleday.

Abrahamsen, D. 1946. *The mind and death of a genius.* New York: Columbia University Press.

Adams, P. 1970. Bisexual conflicts of adolescents with school phobia. *Psychiatry Digest*, 31: 47-49.

———— 1966. School phobia and bisexual conflict. *American Journal of Psychiatry* 123: 541-547.

Adler, A. 1910. Der psychische hermaphroditismus in leben und in der neurose. *Fortschritte der Medizin* 38: 486-493.

Alexander, F. 1933. Bisexual conflict in homosexuality. *Psychiatric Quarterly* 2: 197-201.

Allen, S. 1973. Bisexuality: The best of both worlds. *Spare Rib*, Apr., pp. 25-26.

Altman, D. 1971. *Homosexual: Oppression and liberation.* New York: Outerbridge & Dienstfrey.

Altshuler, K.Z. 1984. On the question of bisexuality. *American Journal of Psychotherapy* 38(4): 484-493.
   *A clinical study of 11 males and 2 females, all self-identified as bisexual, which concludes that bisexuality is displayed only in psychotics (1 subject) or those in transition to homosexuality.

Anderson, S. 1971. *The young bisexuals.* Los Angeles: Centurion Press.

Anxieu, D. 1973, Spring. La Bisexualité dans l'autoanalyse de Freud. *Nouvelle Revue de Psychoanalyse*, p. 7.

Arce, H. 1979. *The secret life of Tyrone Power: The drama of a bisexual in the spotlight*. New York: Morrow.

Arduin. 1900. Die Frauenfrage und die sexuellen Zwischenstufen. *Jahrbuch für sexuellen Zwischenstufen* 2: 211-223.

Arieti, S. ed. 1974-75. *American handbook of psychiatry*. 2nd ed. New York: Basic Books.

Arnaud-Lefoulon, D. 1961. Bisexualité des dieux dans la mythologie hindouiste. *Arcadie* 86: 82-85.

Auerback, S., and C. Moser. 1987. Groups for the wives of gay and bisexual men. *Social Work* 32(4): 321-325.

Bak, R. 1969. The phallic woman: The ubiquitous fantasy in perversions. *Psychoanalytic Quarterly* 38: 516.
*It appears in *Psychoanalytic Study of the Child* 23 (1968): 15-36.

Balint, M. 1963. The younger sister and prince charming. *International Journal of Psychoanalysis* 44: 226-227.

Barr, G. 1985. Chicago Bi-Ways: An informal history. *Journal of Homosexuality* 11(1-2): 231-234.

Bartlett, J. 1966. A bisexual fantasy associated with the testes. *Bulletin of the Psychoanalytic Association of New York* 6(2/3): 23-24.

Basse, L. 1982. *An Uncertain Memory*. New York: Morrow.

Bazin, N. 1974. The concept of androgyny: A working bibliography. *Women's Studies* 2: 217-235.

Bazlin, N. 1977. *Virginia Woolf and the androgynous vision*. New Jersey: Rutgers University Press.

Bell, A.P. 1968. Additional aspects of passivity and female identification in the male. *International Journal of Psychoanalysis* 49 640-647.

Bell, A.P., and M.S. Weinberg. 1978. *Homosexualities: A study of diversity among men and women*. New York: Simon & Schuster.

Bell, A.P., M.S. Weinberg, and S.K. Hammersmith. 1981. *Sexual Preference: Its development in men and women*. Bloomington, IN: Indiana University Press.

Bell-Meltereau, R. 1986. *Hollywood androgyny*. New York: Columbia University Press.

Bem, S. 1974. The measurement of psychological androgyny. *Journal of Consulting and Clinical Psychology* 42: 155-162.

—— 1977. On the utility of alternative procedures for assessing psychological androgyny. *Journal of Consulting and Clinical Psychology* 45: 196-205.

Benedek, T. 1973. *Psychoanalytic investigations: Selected papers*. New York: Times Books.

—— 1959. Sexual functions in women and their disturbance. In *American handbook of psychiatry*, ed. S. Arieti, 727-748. New York: Basic Books.

Berezin, M. 1954. Enuresis and bisexual identification. *Journal of the American Psychoanalytic Association*: 2: 509-513.

Bergenson, R. 1983. *Die Bisexuelle Frau*. Munich: Moewig.

Bieber, I. 1969. The married male homosexual. *Medical aspects of human sexuality* 3(5): 76-84.

Bieler, H., and S. Nichols. 1972. *Dr. Bieler's natural way to sexual health*. Los Angeles: Charles.

Binstock, W. 1973. On the two forms of intimacy. *Journal of the American Psychoanalytic Association* 21: 93-107.

Bird, B. 1958. A study of the bisexual meaning of foreskin. *Journal of the American Psychoanalytic Association* 6: 278-286.

Bird, C. 1968. *Born Female*. New York: Pocket Books.

Bisexual Chic: Anyone goes. 1974. *Newsweek Magazine*, May 24, 90.

Bisexual Lives. 1988. London: Off Pink Publishing.

Bishop, G. 1964. *The bisexuals*. Los Angeles: Century Publishing.

Blair, R. 1974. Counseling concerns and bisexual behavior. *The Homosexual Counseling Journal* 1(2): 26-30.

Blanchard, R. 1985. Typology of male-to-female transsexualism. *Archives of Sexual Behavior* 14(3): 247-261.
*A comparison of bisexual, heterosexual, asexual, and homosexual male-to-female transsexuals.

Blos, P. 1979. *The adolescent passage: Developmental issues*. New York: International Universities Press.

—— 1965. The initial stage of male adolescence. *Psychoanalytic study of the child* 20: 145-164.

Blueher, H. 1912. *Niels Lyhne* von J.P. Jakobsen und das Problem der bisexualität (J.P. Jakobsen's *Niels Lyhne* and the problems of bisexuality). *Imago* 1: 386-400.

Blumstein, P.W., and P. Schwartz. 1976. Bisexual women. In *The social psychology of sex*, ed. J. Wiseman, 154-162. New York: Harper & Row.

—— 1976. Bisexuality in men. *Urban Life* 5: 339-358.

—— 1976. Bisexuality in women. *Archives of Sexual Behavior* 5: 171-181.

—— 1977. Bisexuality: Some social psychological issues. *Journal of Social*

Issues 33: 30-45.

———— 1974. Lesbianism and bisexuality. *Archives of Sexual Behavior* 5: 171-181.

Bode, J. 1976. *View from another closet: Exploring bisexuality in women*. New York: Hawthorn Books.

*Discussion based around interviews with several bisexual women.

Bonaparte, M. 1935. Passivity, masochism, and femininity. *International Journal of Psychoanalysis* 16: 325-333.

Bonaparte, M., A. Freud, and E. Kris, eds. 1954. *Origins of psychoanalysis: Letters to Wilhelm Fliess, drafts, and notes: 1887-1902*. New York: Basic Books.

Boswell, J. 1980. *Christianity, social tolerance and homosexuality*. Chicago: University of Chicago Press.

Bozett, F. 1981. Gay fathers: Identity conflict resolution through integrative sanctioning. *Alternative Lifestyles* 4: 90-101.

Bram, J.R. 1979. Sex reversal in the ancient world. In *Psychosexual imperatives: Their role in identity formation*, ed. M.C. Nelson and J. Ikenberry, 91-106. New York: Human Sciences Press.

Breger, L. 1981. *Freud's unfinished journey*. London: Routledge & Kegan Paul.

Breitner, B. 1951. *Das Problem der Bisexualität*. Wein: Verlag Wilhelm Maundrich.

Breslow, N., L. Evans, and J. Langley. 1986. Comparisons among heterosexual, bisexual, and homosexual male sado-masochists. *Journal of Homosexuality* 13(1): 83-107

Bressler, L.C., and A.D. Lavender. 1986. Sexual fulfillment of heterosexual, bisexual, and homosexual women. *Journal of Homosexuality* 12(3-4): 109-122.

*Suggests that increasing an individual's knowledge of all sexual orientations will likewise increase her sexual fulfillment, regardless of orientation.

Brody, E. 1978. Intimacy and the fantasy of becoming both sexes. *Journal of the American Academy of Psychoanalysis* 6: 521-531.

Brody, J. 1974. Bisexual life-style appears to be spreading, and not necessarily among swingers. *New York Times*, Mar. 24, p. 57.

*Based on a study done at the University of Washington.

Broughton, J. 1977. *The androgyne journal*. Oakland, CA: Scrimshaw Press.

Brown, R. 1965. *Social Psychology*. New York: Free Press.

*An excellent commentary on Freud's concept of identification vis-à-vis bisexuality, pp. 278-279.

Brownfain, J.J. 1985. A study of the married bisexual male: Paradox and resolution. *Journal of Homosexuality* 11(1-2): 173-188.

Bryan, D. 1930. Bisexuality. *International Journal of Psychoanalysis* 11: 150-166.

Burgess, P. 1968. *Confessions of a married man.* New York: Lanier Books.

Burnside, J. 1963. Bisexuality and its possiblities as a way of life. *One Magazine*, Aug., pp. 6-9.

Buzzacott, F., and M. Wymore. 1912. *Bi-sexual man, or evolution of the sexes.* Chicago: M.A. Donahue.

Campbell, C. 1958. *Induced delusions: The psychopathy of Freudism.* Chicago: Regent House.

*One chapter attacks Freud's concept of bisexuality.

Caprio, F. 1955. *The adequate male.* New York: Medical Research Press.

Carledge, S., and J. Ryan, eds. 1983. *Sex and love: New thoughts on old contradictions.* Canada: The Women's Press.

*Includes a chapter on bisexuality by Debora Gregory.

Carpenter, E. 1919. *Intermediate types among primitive folk.* 2nd ed. London: Allen & Unwin. (Originally published in 1914.)

Carrier, J.M. 1985. Mexican male bisexuality. *Journal of Homosexuality* 11(1-2): 75-85.

Cass, V. 1979. Homosexual identity formation: A theoretical model. *Journal of Homosexuality* 4: 219-233.

Cauldwell, D. 1948. *Bisexuality in patterns of human behavior: A study of individuals who indulge in both heterosexual and homosexual practices, with comparative data on hermaphrodites, the human intersex.* Girard, KS: Haldeman-Julius Publications.

Chartier, D.A. 1982. Freud et Haizmann: L'artiste et l'analyste. (Freud and Haizmann: Artist and analyst.) *Psychologie Medicale* 14(9): 1363-1366.

*Highlights links between bisexuality and creativity. — T.G.

Childs, E. 1976. Women's sexuality: A feminist view. In *Female psychology: The emerging self*, S. Cox, ed. Chicago: Science Research Associates.

Christy, R. 1968. *The intermediate gender: The sex that can't make up its mind.* Van Nuys, CA: Triumph.

*Possibly "The Indeterminate Gender"? Listed as such in various sources.

Churchill, W. 1967. *Homosexual behavior among males: A cross-cultural and cross-species investigation.* New York: Hawthorn Books.

Clark, D., ed. 1973. Symposium: AC/DC: The bisexual. *The Humanist* 33(4): 15-20.

Coleman, E. 1987. Assessment of sexual orientation. *Journal of Homosexuality* 14(1-2): 9-24.
  *Proposes a complex, nine-dimensional model for sexual orientation.
——— 1981/1982. Bisexual and gay men in heterosexual marriage: Conflicts and resolutions in therapy. *Journal of Homosexuality* 7(2/3): 93-103.
——— 1985. Bisexual women in marriages. *Journal of Homosexuality* 11(1-2): 87-99.
——— 1985. Integration of bisexuality and marriage. *Journal of Homosexuality* 11(1-2): 189-207.
Collins, L.E., and N. Zimmerman. 1983. Homosexual and bisexual issues. *Family Therapy Collections* 5: 82-100.
  *Discusses (1) mixed-orientation couples and (2) families with a bisexual or homosexual child.
Colton, N. 1954. Salvation: An expression of bisexuality. *Bulletin of the Philadelphia Association of Psychoanalysts* 4: 36-37.
Comfort, A. 1972. *The joy of sex.* New York: Crown.
——— 1974. *More joy of sex.* New York: Crown.
Cook, E.P. 1985. *Psychological androgyny.* New York: Pergamon.
Coons, F. 1972. Ambisexuality as an alternative adaptation. *Journal of the American College Health Association* 21: 142-144.
Coriat, I. 1917. Hermaphroditic dreams. *Psychoanalytic Review* 40: 88-92.
Corvo, B. 1953. *The desire and pursuit of the whole.* New York: New Directions.
Cory, D., and J. LeRo. 1963. *The homosexual and his society.* New York: Citadel Press.
Cucchiari, S. 1981. The gender revolution and the transition from bisexual horde to patrilocal band. In *Sexual meanings,* ed. S. Ortner and H. Whitehead: 31-79. New York: Cambridge University Press.
Daniel, D.G., V. Abernethy, and W.R. Oliver. 1984. Correlations between female sex roles and attitudes toward male sexual dysfunction in thirty women. *Journal of Sex and Marital Therapy* 10(3): 160-169.
  *Compared 15 heterosexual feminist women to 15 bisexual feminist women and found that both feminism and bisexuality are associated with a less demanding and critical response to male sexual performance.
Dank, B. 1972. Why homosexuals marry women. *Medical aspects of human sexuality* 6: 614-627.
Darwin, C. 1871. *The descent of man, and selection in relation to sex.* Vol. 1. London: John Murray.
David, C. 1975. La bisexualité psychique: Éléments d'une réevaluation.

Revue Française de Psychoanalyse 39: 713-757.

——— 1977. Psychic bisexuality: Clinical and theoretical considerations. *International Psychoanalytic Association Newsletter* 9(1):33.

Davis, C. 1968. *AC/DC*. Los Angeles: Classic Publications.

Deb, S. 1979. On bisexuality: An overview. *Samiska* 33(2): 53-57.

De Cecco, J.P. 1981. Definition and meaning of sexual orientation. *Journal of Homosexuality* 6(4): 51-67.

——— ed. 1984. *Bisexual and homosexual identities: Critical clinical issues*. (Journal of Homosexuality Series: No.4.) New York: Haworth Press.

De Cecco, J.P., and M.G. Shively, eds. 1984. *Bisexual and homosexual identities: Critical theoretical issues*. (Journal of Homosexuality Series: Vol. 9, No. 2-3.) New York: Haworth Press.

Delcourt, M. 1961. *Hermaphrodite: The bisexual figure in myth and ritual*. London: Studio Books. (Originally published in French, 1956.)

De Lora, J., and C. Warren. 1977. *Understanding sexual interaction*. Boston: Houghton Mifflin.

Denniston, R. 1980. Ambisexuality in animals. In *Homosexual behavior*, ed. J. Marmor, 25-40. New York: Basic Books.

De River, J.P. 1958. *Crime and the sexual psychopath*. Springfield, IL: C.C. Thomas.

Dervin, D. 1980. Rainbow, phoenix, and plumed serpent: D.H. Lawrence's great composite symbols and their vicissitudes. *Psychoanalytic Review* 67: 515-541.

Deutsch, H. 1968. Bisexuality and immortality in the Dionysius myth. *Psychoanalytic Quarterly* 37: 321-322.

——— 1944. The psychology of women. New York: Grune & Stratton.

——— 1967. *Selected problems of adolescence with special emphasis on group formation*. New York: International Universities Press.

Devereux, G. 1982. *Femme et mythe*. Paris: Flammarion.

Dickes, R. 1971. Factors in the development of male homosexuality. In *The unconscious today*, ed. M. Kanzet, 25-273. New York: International Universities Press.

Dixon, D. 1985. Perceived sexual satisfaction and marital happiness of bisexual and heterosexual swinging husbands. *Journal of Homosexuality* 11(1-2): 209-222.

Dixon, J.K. 1984. The commencement of bisexual activity in swinging married women over age thirty. *Journal of Sex Research* 20(1): 71-90.

——— 1985. Sexuality and relationship changes in married females following the commencement of bisexual activity. *Journal of Homosexuality* 11(1-2): 115-133.

Doucet, P. 1988. Pruritus ani. *International Journal of Psychoanalysis* 69(3): 409-417

*Bisexuality analyzed in a 30-year-old male subject, focusing on pruritus ani.

Douglas, J. 1970. *Bisexuality*. London: Canova Press, Ltd.

Eglinton, J.Z. 1965. *Greek love*. New York: Oliver Layton Press.

Ehrhardt, A.A. 1985. Sexual orientation after prenatal exposure to exogenous estrogen. *Archives of Sexual Behavior* 14(1): 57-77.

*Studies effects of the now-illegal synthetic hormone DES in relation to the child's sexual orientation.

Eissler, K.R. 1971. *Talent and genius: The fictitious case of Tausk contra Freud*. New York: Quadrangle.

*See also listing for P. Roazen.

Ellenberger, H. F. 1970. *The discovery of the unconscious*. New York: Basic Books.

Engel, J.W., and M. Saracino. 1986. Love preferences and ideals: A comparison of homosexual, bisexual, and heterosexual groups. *Contemporary Family Therapy: An International Journal* 8(3): 241-250.

Evan, D., and A.M. Zeiss. 1984. Catastrophe theory: A topological reconceptualization of sexual orientation. *New Ideas in Psychology* 2(3): 235-251.

*Discusses the varying nature of one's sexuality in light of the sequential nature of relationships.

Faithfull, T.J. 1927. *Bisexuality: An essay on extroversion and introversion*. London: John Bale, Sons & Danielson, Ltd.

Falk, R. 1975. *Women loving: A journey toward becoming an independent woman*. New York: Random House.

*Discusses women's love with both sexes, but eschews all labels, including "bisexual."

Fast, I. 1978. Developments in gender identity: The original matrix. *International Review of Psychoanalysis* 5(3): 265-273.

Fast, J., and H. Wells. 1975. *Bisexual Living*. New York: Evans.

*Includes several interviews. Much of the book is spent determining whether or not the interview subjects are "really bi."

Fineman, J. 1979. Psychoanalysis, bisexuality, and the difference between the sexes. In *Psychosexual imperatives: Their role in identity formation*, ed. M.C. Nelson and J. Ikenberry, 109-145. New York: Human Sciences Press.

Fisher, P. 1972. *The gay mystique: The myth and reality*. New York: Stein & Day.

Fissinger, L. 1987. Both sides of bisexuality. *Playgirl*, Oct., 84-87.

    *Interviewed women involved in some of the organized bisexual networks: interview subjects later reported that they felt that they had been treated fairly in the article.

Flygare, T.J. 1985. The firing of a bisexual counselor: Unresolved constitutional issues. *Phi Delta Kappan* 66(9): 648-649.

Fodor, N. 1954. Dreams of masculine regret. In *The homosexual*, ed. A.M. Krich 25-28. New York: Citadel Press.

——— 1946. The search for the beloved. *Psychiatric Quarterly* 20: 294-306.

Ford, C.S., and F.A. Beach. 1951. *Patterns of sexual behavior*. New York: Harper.

Forman, M. 1976. The bisexual phallic narcissistic phase of development, sexual identity and the cohesive. Paper presented at the sixth Regional Conference of the Chicago Psychoanalytic Society, Chicago, IL.

Fraser-Harris, D.F. 1933. Bisexual mentality. *Hibbert Journal* 31: 571-581.

Freud, S. 1937. Analysis terminable and interminable. In *The standard edition of the complete psychological works of Sigmund Freud* Vol. 23, Part 8, ed. and trans. J. Strachey, London: Hogarth Press, 1961.

——— 1923. Femininity. In *The standard edition of the complete psychological works of Sigmund Freud*, Vol. 22, 112-135, ed. and trans. J. Strachey, London: Hogarth Press, 1961.

——— 1923. Hysterical phantasies and their relation to bisexuality. In *The standard edition of the complete psychological works of Sigmund Freud*, Vol. 9, 157-160, ed. and trans. J. Strachey, London: Hogarth Press, 1961.

——— 1960. *The letters of Sigmund Freud*, ed. E. Freud, New York: Basic Books. *See especially the portion of letter 122, pp. 250-251, written to Karl Kraus, dealing with the Fleiss/Weininger/Svoboda controversy; and see letter 209, pp. 350-352, to Fritz Wittels, written 1924, about Wittels' Freud biography and the Fliess controversy.

——— 1923. Notes on a case of obsessional neurosis. In *The standard edition of the complete psychological works of Sigmund Freud*, Vol. 10, 153-320, ed. and trans. J. Strachey, London: Hogarth Press, 1961.

——— 1923. The psychoanalysis of a case of homosexuality in a woman. In *The standard edition of the complete psychological works of Sigmund Freud*, Vol. 18, 146-154, ed. and trans. J. Strachey, London: Hogarth Press, 1961.

——— 1923. Psychoanalytic notes upon an autobiographical account of a case of paranoia. In *The standard edition of the complete psychological works of Sigmund Freud*, Vol. 12, 9-82, ed. and trans. J. Strachey, London: Hogarth

Press, 1961.

———— 1905. Three essays on the theory of sexuality. In *The standard edition of the complete psychological works of Sigmund Freud*, Vol. 7, inclusive, ed. and trans. J. Strachey, London: Hogarth Press, 1961.

Freund, K. 1974. Male homosexuality. An analysis of the pattern. In *Understanding homosexuality: Its biological and psychological bases*, ed. J.A. Loraine, 25-81. New York: American Elsevier.

Freund, K., and R. Langevin. 1976. Bisexuality in homosexual pedophilia. *Archives of Sexual Behavior* 5: 415-424.

Freund, K., H. Scher, S. Chan, and M. Ben-Aron. 1982. Experimental analysis of pedophilia. *Behavior Research and Therapy* 20: 105-112.

Friedman, S. 1976. On the umbilicus as a bisexual genital. *Psychoanalytic Quarterly* 45: 296-298.

Frosch, J. 1981. The role of unconscious homosexuality in the paranoid constellation. *Psychoanalytic Quarterly* 50: 587-613.

Gagnon, J. 1977. *Human Sexualities*. Glenview, IL: Scott, Foresman.

Galland, V.R. 1975. Bisexual Women. Doctoral diss., California School of Professional Psychology. *Dissertation Abstracts International*, Vol. 36 (6-B), 3037-3038.

Galt, W.E. 1943. The male-female dichotomy in human behavior: A psychobiological evaluation. *Psychiatry Journal of the Biology and Pathology of Interpersonal Relations* 6(1): 1-14.

Gault, O., and R.M. Smith. 1961. *Sex clinic*. Hollywood, CA: All Star Classic Books.

Gay America. 1983. *Newsweek*, Aug. 8, 30-36

Gebhard, P.H. 1972. Incidence of overt homosexuality in the U.S. and Western Europe. In *NIMH task force on homosexuality: Final report and papers*, ed. J.M. Livingood (#HSM 72-9116.) Rockville, MD: Department of Health, Education, and Welfare.

Gebhard, P.H., and A.B. Johnson. 1979. *The Kinsey data: Marginal tabulations of the 1938-1963 interviews conducted by the Institute for Sex Research*. Philadelphia: W.B. Saunders.

Gelman, D. 1987. A perilous double love life. *Newsweek* 110: July 13, 44-46. *Infamous in organized bi communities. Purporting to be about bisexuals, the article focuses on closeted bisexual men with AIDS. Some interview subjects claim to have been misquoted, or to have had their words misleadingly taken out of context.

Gilmore, M.M., and D.D. Gilmore. 1979. Machismo: A psychodramatic approach. *Journal of Psychological Anthropology* 23: 281-299.

Giraldo, O. 1982. Mas alla de la heterosexualidad (Beyond heterosexuality). *Avances en Psycologia Clinica Latinoamericana* 1: 79-94.

*An overview of bisexuality.

Gochros, H.L. 1978. Counseling gay husbands. *Journal of Sex and Marital Therapy* 5: 142-151.

Gochros, J.S. 1989. *When husbands come out of the closet*. New York: Haworth.

———— 1985. Wives' reactions to learning that their husbands are bisexual. *Journal of Homosexuality* 11(1-2): 101-113.

Goldwert, M. 1985. Mexican machismo: The flight from femininity. *Psychoanalytic Review* 72(1): 161-169.

*See also Carrier's related article 1985.

Gonsiorek, J.C., W. Paul, J.D. Weinrich, and M.E. Hotvedt, eds. 1982. *Homosexuality: Social, psychological, and biological issues*. Beverly Hills: Sage Publications.

Gottman, J.M. 1979. *Marital interaction: Experimental investigations*. Chicago: Academic Press.

Goy, R.W. 1974. Comparative aspects of bisexuality in mammals. Paper presented at the Research Workshop on Future Directions in Research in Human Sexuality. State University of New York, Stony Brook, NY. Available from Bloomington, IN: Alfred C. Kinsey Institute (mimeo, 24 pp.).

Grant, G.G. 1986. Loving a bisexual man. *Essence* 17: Nov., 12.

*As with most popular-magazine treatments of the subject, this one essentially warns women away from bisexual men. Aimed at a black audience.

Graves, A. 1942. *The eclipse of a mind*. New York: Medical Journal Press.

Greenacre, P. 1952. *Trauma, growth, and personality*. New York: Norton.

Greenson, R. 1964. Bisexuality and gender identity. *International Journal of Psychoanalysis* 45: 217-219.

Grossman, W.I. 1976. Discussion of "Freud and female sexuality." *International Journal of Psychoanalysis* 57: 301-306.

Guttman, S.A. 1955. Bisexuality in symbolism. *Journal of the American Psychoanalytic Association* 3: 280-284.

Halfpenny, P., and J. Cotterill. 1986. Who calls friend? *British Journal of Guidance and Counseling* 14(2): 154-167.

*A study of calls made to a gay counseling agency. Suggests that such a service is most successful when caller's and counselor's sexualities are matched (i.e. bi to bi, gay to gay, etc.).

Hansen, C.E., and A. Evans. 1985. Bisexuality reconsidered: An idea in pursuit of a definition. *Journal of Homosexuality* 11(1-2): 1-6.

Harley, M. 1963. A secret in prepuberty (its sexual aspects). *Psychoanalytic Quarterly* 32: 616-617.

Harriman, P. 1964. *Bisexuality: Normal or not?* North Hollywood: Dominion.

Harris, D.A. 1977. Social-psychological characteristics of ambisexuals. Doctoral diss., University of Tennessee, Knoxville, TN. Available from University Microfilms, Ann Arbor, Michigan, order no. 78-2004, 525.

Harrison, B.G. 1974. Sexual chic, sexual fascism, and sexual confusion. *New York Magazine*, Apr., 31-36.

Harry, J., and W. De Vall. 1978. *The social organization of gay males*. New York: Praeger.

Hartman, J.J., and G.S. Gilbard. 1973. Bisexual fantasy and group process. *Contemporary Psychoanalysis* 93: 303-326.

Harwell, J.L. 1976. Bisexuality: Persistent lifestyle or transitional state? Doctoral diss., International University, Independence, MO. Available from University Microfilms, Ann Arbor, Michigan. Order #76-22, 384.

Hathaway, B. 1974. Bisexuality: An annotated bibliography. Available at Kinsey Institute for Sex Research.

Hatterer, M.S. 1974. The problems of women married to homosexual men. *American Journal of Psychiatry* 131: 275-278.

Heilbrun, C.G. 1973. *Towards a recognition of bisexuality*. New York: Knopf.

Heller, A.C. 1987. Is there a man in your man's life? What every girl should know about the bisexual guy. *Mademoiselle*, Jul.
*A vicious and sensationalistic attack of bisexual men, with horror-moviesque paragraph headers like "They lead two lives."

Helmreich, R.L., J.T. Spence, and C.K. Holahan. 1979. Psychological androgyny and sex role flexibility: A test of two hypotheses. *Journal of Personality and Social Psychology* 37: 1631-1644.

Henry, G.W. 1955. *All the sexes: A study of masculinity and femininity*. New York: Rinehart.

Herdt, G.H. 1984. A comment on cultural attributes and fluidity of bisexuality. *Journal of Homosexuality* 10(3-4): 53-61.

Hill, I., ed. 1987. *The Bisexual Spouse*. Virginia: Barlina Books.

Hinkle, B.M. 1922. *The re-creating of the individual*. New York: Harcourt Brace.

Hirschfeld, M. 1906. *Die gestohlene bisexualität*. Vienna: (n.p.).

——— 1912. *Naturgesetze der liebe* (The nature of love). Berlin: Pulvermacher.

(Published earlier in Leipzig in 1895 and 1906.)

Hodges, A., and D. Hutter. 1979. *With downcast gays: Aspects of homosexual self-oppression*. 2nd ed. Toronto: Pink Triangle Press.

Hoffman, M. 1976. *The gay world: Male homosexuality and the social creation of evil*. New York: Basic Books.

Horney, K. 1967. *Feminine psychology*. New York: Norton.

Hucker, S., R. Langevin, G. Wortzman, J. Bain, L. Handy, J. Chambers, and S. Wright. 1986. Neuropsychological impairment in pedophiles. *Canadian Journal of Behavioural Science* 18(4): 440-448.
*A study and comparison of 15 heterosexual, 14 homosexual, and 10 bisexual male pedophiles.

Humphreys, L. 1970. *Tearoom trade: Impersonal sex in public places*. New York: Aldine.

Humphreys, L., and B. Miller. 1970. Identities in the emerging gay culture. In *Homosexual behavior: A modern re-appraisal*, ed. J. Marmor, New York: Basic Books.

Hunt, M.B. 1974. *Sexual behavior in the 1970s*. Chicago: Playboy Press.

Hurwood, B.J. 1974. *The bisexuals*. Greenwich: Fawcett.

Hutchins, L. 1988. Biatribe: A feminist bisexual politic for change. *Off Our Backs*. Feb.

Imielinski, K. 1970. *Milieubedingte einstehung der homo- und bisexualität: Eine theorie der geschlechtsorientierung* (Situational origin of homosexuality and bisexuality: A theory of sexual orientation). Munich and Basel: Ernst Reinhardt Verlag.
*This appears to be a translation to German of the original Polish work. There is no English translation, but the German edition is still available.

Institute for Sex Research Information Service. 1979. *Bisexuality*. (Annotated bibliography). Available from the Alfred Kinsey Institute, Bloomington, IN.

Istvan, J. 1983. Effects of sexual orientation on interpersonal judgement. *Journal of Sex Research* 19(2): 173-191.
*Finds that heterosexually-tending subjects were seen as more likable, sexually desirable, sexually active, and better work partners.

Jardine, J., and S. Whyte. 1971. *The bisexual female*. Los Angeles: Centurion Press.

Jay, K., and A. Young. 1979. *The gay report*. New York: Summit.

Kalcheim, C., H. Szechtman, and Y. Koch. 1981. Bisexual behavior in male rats treated neonatally with antibodies to luteinizing hormone-releasing hormone. *Journal of Comparative and Physiological Psychology* 95(1): 36-44.

Kantrowitz, A. 1977. Bosom buddies. *The Advocate.* May 4, 31-32.

Kaplan, A., and M.A. Sedney. 1980. *Psychology and sex roles: An androgynous perspective.* Boston: Little, Brown.

Kardiner, A., A. Karush, and L. Ovesey. 1959. A methodological study of Freudian theory. *Journal of Nervous and Mental Diseases* 129: 11-19, 133-143, 207-221, 341-346.

Karlen, A. 1971. *Sexuality and homosexuality: A new view.* New York: Norton.

Katan, M. 1955. Those wrecked by success, bisexual conflicts, and ego defense. *The Psychoanalytic Quarterly* 24: 477-478.

Katz, S. 1987. Straight woman, bisexual man: High-risk couple? *Chatelaine,* Oct., 69.

Kelly, G.F. 1974. Bisexuality and youth culture. *The Homosexual Counseling Journal* 1(2): 16-25.

Kempf, E.J. 1949. Bisexual factors in curable schizophrenia. *Journal of Abnormal and Social Psychology* 44: 414-419.

———— 1945. Ontogeny of bisexual differentiation in man. *Journal of Clinical Psychopathology* 7: 213.

Kestenberg, J., and H. Marcus. 1979. Hypothetical monosex and bisexuality. In *Psychosexual imperatives: Their role in identity formation,* ed. M.C. Nelson and J. Ikenberry, New York: Human Sciences Press.

Khan, M., and R. Masud. 1979. *Alienation in perversion.* London: Hogarth Press.

———— 1974. Ego orgasm and bisexual love. *International Review of Psychoanalysis* 1: 143-149.

Kiernan, J. G. 1884. Insanity: Lecture XXVI — Sexual perversion. *Detroit Lancet* 7: 481-484.

———— 1891. Psychological aspects of the sexual appetite. *The Alienist and Neurologist* 12: 188-219.

Kinsey, A.C., W.B. Pomeroy, C.E. Martin, and P.E. Gebhard. 1953. *Sexual behavior in the human female.* Philadelphia: W.B. Saunders.

Kinsey, A.C., W.B. Pomeroy, and C.E. Martin. 1948. *Sexual behavior in the human male.* Philadelphia: W.B. Saunders.

Kisker, G.W. 1972. *The disorganized personality,* 2nd ed. New York: McGraw-Hill.

Klein, F. 1980. Are you sure you're heterosexual? or homosexual? or even bisexual? *Forum* (now *Penthouse Forum*), Dec., 41-45.

———— 1978. *The bisexual option: A concept of 100% intimacy.* New York: Arbor

House.

*A seminal book in the study of bisexuality. One of the first full-length books viewing the subject in a positive light. Includes the results of an informal survey of 150 participants in New York's Bisexual Forum, an early support group.

Klein, F., B. Sepekoff, and T.J. Wolf. 1985. Sexual orientation: A multi-variable dynamic process. *Journal of Homosexuality* 11(1-2): 35-49.

Klein, F., and T.J. Wolf, eds. 1985. *Bisexualities: Theory and research.* New York: Haworth Press. (First published in *Journal of Homosexuality* 11(1-2).)

*Also published (and available at a lower price) under the title: *Two lives to lead: bisexuality in men and women.* New York: Harrington Park Press (a division of Haworth Press).

Kleinberg, S. 1980. *Alienated affections: Being gay in America.* New York: St. Martin's Press.

Klemsrud, J. 1974. The bisexuals. *New York Magazine,* Apr., 37-38.

Knauft, B.M. 1986. Text and social practice: Narrative "longing" and bisexuality among the Gebusi of New Guinea. *Ethos* 14(3): 252-281.

Knox, L. 1974. The bisexual phenomenon. *Viva Magazine,* Jul., 42-45.

Kohn, B., and A. Matusow. 1980. *Barry and Alice: Portrait of a bisexual marriage.* New York: Prentice-Hall.

*An intensely personal account of a marriage in which both participants discovered and dealt with their bisexuality in the years following their wedding.

Korber, H. 1913. Die bisexualität als Grundlage der Sexualforschung (Bisexuality as a basis for sexual research). *Neue Generation* 9: 73.

Krafft-Ebing, R. von. 1965. *Psychopathia sexualis.* London: Staples Press.

*The 10th edition was published in London by Rebman in 1899.

Kraus, Julius. 1906. Otto Weininger, plagiarist. *Die Wage* 43: 970.

Krich, A.M., ed. 1954. *The homosexuals.* New York: Citadel Press.

Krim, S. 1968. *Views of a near-sighted cannoneer.* New York: Dutton.

Kris, A.O. 1988. Some clinical applications of the distinctions between divergent and convergent conflicts. *International Journal of Psychoanalysis* 69(3): 431-441.

*A case study of a neurotic male bisexual.

Kubie, L.S. 1974. The drive to become both sexes. *Psychoanalytic Quarterly* 43: 349-426.

Lampli-De Groot, J. 1967. On obstacles in the way of psychoanalytic cure. *Psychoanalytic Study of the Child* 22: 20-35.

Lang, T. 1971. *The difference between a man and a woman.* New York: John Day.

Laplanche, J. 1974. Panel on hysteria today. *International Journal of Psychoanalysis* 5: 198-212.

Latham, J.D., and G.D. White. 1978. Coping with homosexual expression within heterosexual marriages: Five case studies. *Journal of Sex and Marital Therapy* 4: 198-212.

LaTorre, R.A. 1979. *Sexual identity: Implications for mental health.* Chicago: Nelson-Hall.

LaTorre, R.A., and K. Wendenburg. 1983. Psychological characteristics of bisexual, heterosexual and homosexual women. *Journal of Homosexuality* 9(1): 87-97.

Lebzeltern, G. 1982. Zu Unrecht vergessene Freud-Briefe. (Some letters of Freud, wrongfully forgotten). *Dynamische Psychiatrie* 15(3-4): 97-113.
*Some letters on bisexuality sent to Magnus Hirschfeld.

A lesbian encounter. 1975. *Human Response* 1(7): 34-40.

Lewis, S.G. 1974. Bisexuals are "healthy," researchers conclude. *The Advocate,* Oct. 23, 20.

Limentani, A. 1979. Clinical types of homosexuality. In *Sexual deviation* 2nd ed., ed. I. Rosen, 195-205. New York: Oxford University Press.

———— 1976. Object choice and actual bisexuality. *International Journal of Psychoanalytic Psychotherapy* 5: 205-218.
*Originally appeared as Le choix d'objet dans la bisexualité actuelle, *Revue Française de Psychoanalyse,* 1975, 5: 857-868.

Lippert, G.P. 1986. Excessive concern about AIDS in two bisexual men. *Canadian Journal of Psychiatry* 31(1): 63-65.

Loewenstein, S.F. 1985. On the diversity of love object orientations among women. *Journal of Social Work and Human Sexuality* 3(2-3): 7-24.
*Many of the subjects in this study shifted within the homosexual-heterosexual continuum during their lifetimes, validating bisexuality as an authentic separate category.

Lorand, S. 1931. *Morbid personality.* New York: Knopf.

Losso, R., and S. Morici. 1988. El vacio identificatorio. Un abordaje psicoanalitico de dos pacientes intersexuados. (The identity vacuum: A psychoanalytic approach to two intersexual patients). *Revista de Psicoanalisis* 45(3): 645-672.
*Case studies of two young subjects with intersexual genitals, their psychological development, and effects felt by their families. In Spanish.

Lourea, D.N. 1985. Psycho-social issues related to counseling bisexuals.

Journal of Homosexuality 11(1-2): 51-62.

Lynne, D. 1967. *The bisexual woman.* New York: Midweek.

Macalpine, I., and R.A. Hunter. 1955. *Daniel Paul Schreber: Memoirs of my nervous illness.* London: Dawson.

MacDonald, A.P. 1981. An annotated subject-indexed bibliography of research on bisexuality, lesbianism and male homosexuality 1975-1978. *Catalog of Selected Documents in Psychology* 11(16): Ms. 2206.

————— 1983. A little bit of lavender goes a long way: A critique of research on sexual orientation. *Journal of Sex Research* 19: 94-100.

*Asserts that the practice of lumping bisexuals with homosexuals in research should be discontinued in light of significant differences between the two groups.

————— 1984. Reactions to issues concerning sexual orientations, identities, preferences, and choices. *Journal of Homosexuality* 10(3-4): 23-27.

*States that "unomania" (preoccupation with single causes), which is so common in homosexual research, is especially inappropriate to bisexual research.

MacInnes, C. 1973. *Loving them both: A study in bisexuality and bisexuals.* London: Martin Bran & O'Keefe.

Maddox, B. 1982. *Married and gay: What happens when a gay man marries a lesbian?* New York: Harcourt Brace Jovanovich.

Malone, J. 1980. *Straight women/gay men: A special relationship.* New York: Dial Press.

Margold, J. 1974. Bisexuality: The newest sex-style. *Cosmopolitan*, Jun., 189-192.

Markus, E. 1981. An examination of psychological adjustment and sexual preference in the female. Doctoral diss., University of Missouri (1980). *Dissertation Abstracts International* 41: 4338-A.

Marmor, J. ed. 1965. *Sexual inversion: The multiple roots of homosexuality.* New York: Basic Books.

Masters, W.H., and V.E. Johnson. 1979. *Homosexuality in Perspective.* Boston: Little, Brown.

Matteson, D.R. 1985. Bisexual men in marriage: Is a positive homosexual identity and stable marriage possible? *Journal of Homosexuality* 11(1-2): 149-171.

Matthews, J. 1969. Bisexuality in the male. *The Journal of Sex Research* 5: 126-129.

McCary, J.L. 1971. *Sexual myths and fallacies.* New York: Van Nostrand Reinhold.

McConaghy, N. 1978. Heterosexual experience, marital status, and orientation of homosexual males. *Archives of Sexual Behavior* 7: 575-582.

McConaghy, N., M.S. Armstrong, P.C. Birrell, and N. Buhrich. 1979. The incidence of bisexual feelings and opposite sex behavior in medical students. *Journal of Nervous and Mental Disease* 167: 685-688.

McMurtie, D.C. 1913. The theory of bisexuality: A review and critique. *Lancet Clinic* 109: 370-372.

Mead, M. 1975. Bisexuality: What's it all about? *Redbook Magazine*, Jan.

Melukx, I.U. 1976. Discussion of Freud and female sexuality. *International Journal of Psychoanalysis* 75: 307-310.

Mendola, M. 1980. *The Mendola Report: A new look at gay couples*. New York: Crown.

Meyerson, S. 1975. *Adolescence: The crisis of adjustment*. Winchester, MA: Allen & Unwin.

Mishaan, C. 1985. The bisexual scene in New York City. *Journal of Homosexuality* 11(1-2): 223-225.

Money, J. 1977. Bisexual, homosexual and heterosexual: Society, law and medicine. *Journal of Homosexuality* 2: 229-233.

——— 1986. Homosexual genesis, outcome studies, and a nature/nurture paradigm shift. *American Journal of Social Psychiatry* 6(2): 95-98.

——— 1978. Human hermaphroditism. In *Human sexuality in four perspectives*, ed. F.A. Beach, 62-86. Baltimore: Johns Hopkins University Press.

——— 1980. *Love and love sickness*. Baltimore: Johns Hopkins University Press.

——— 1974. The new bisexual. *Time Magazine*. May 13, 79-80.

——— 1972. Pubertal hormones and homosexuality, bisexuality and heterosexuality. In *National Institute of Mental Health Task Force on Homosexuality: Final Report and Background Papers*. Washington D.C.: U.S. Government Printing Office.

——— 1987. Sin, sickness, or status? Homosexual gender identity and psychoneuroendocrinology. *American Psychologist* 42(4): 384-399.
*Discusses the role of prenatal hormonization of the brain as compared to postnatal socialization as determining factors of sexual orientation.

——— 1974. Two names, two wardrobes, two personalities. *Journal of Homosexuality* 1: 65-70.

Money, J., and A.A. Ehrhardt. 1972. *Man and woman/boy and girl*. Baltimore: Johns Hopkins University Press.

Money, J., and V.G. Lewis. 1987. Bisexually concordant, heterosexually and homosexually discordant. *Psychiatry* 50: 97-111.

Money, J., and P. Tucker. 1975. *Sexual signatures: On being a man or a woman.* Boston: Little, Brown.

Money-Kryle, R. 1952. *The development of sexual impulses.* London: Routledge & Kegan Paul. (Original work published 1932.)

Moore, B.E. 1976. Freud and female sexuality: A current view. *International Journal of Psychoanalysis* 57: 287-300.

Murphy, T.F. 1984. Freud reconsidered: Bisexuality, homosexuality, and moral judgment. *Journal of Homosexuality* 9(2-3): 65-77.
    *Suggests that Freud's moral stances prohibited him from seeing bisexuality as a valid adult orientation or homosexuality as anything other than arrested development.

Murphy, W. F. 1965. *The tactics of psychotherapy.* New York: International University Press.

Myer, L. 1976. Bisexual behavior. Indiana University, Alfred A. Kinsey Institute, Bloomington, IN.

Myerson, A., and R. Neustadt. 1942. Bisexuality and male homosexuality: Their biological and medical aspects. *Clinic* 1: 932-957.

Nacke, P. 1906. Some psychiatric experiences in support of bisexual vestiges in mankind. *Jahrbuch für Sexualzwischenstufen* 8: 583-603.
    *This is apparently available only in the German original.

Nahas, R., and M. Turley. 1979. *The new couple: Women and gay men.* New York: Seaview Books.

Narlett, J.W. 1966. A bisexual fantasy associated with the testes. *Bulletin of the Psychoanalytic Association of New York* 6: 23-24.

Nelson, M.C., and J. Ikenberry, eds. 1979. *Psychosexual imperatives: Their role in identity formation.* New York: Human Sciences Press.
    *See contributions by Bram, Fineman, and Kestenberg and Marcus.

Newman, L.E., and R.F. Stoller. 1969. Spider symbolism and bisexuality. *Journal of the American Psychoanalytic Association* 17: 862-872.

Nunberg, H. 1968. Homosexuality, magic and aggression. *International Journal of Psychoanalysis* 19: 1-16.

——— 1949. *Problems of bisexuality as reflected in circumcision.* London: Imago.

Nurius, P.S. 1983. Mental health implications of sexual orientation. *Journal of Sex Research* 19(2): 119-136.
    *Correlated asexuality, bisexuality, homosexuality, and heterosexuality with: depression, self-esteem, sexual discord, and marital discord. Found that the only significant difference correlated between the groups was in depression, accounting for less than two percent of its total variance.

O'Flaherty, W.D. 1980. *Women, androgynes, and other mythical beasts.* Chicago and London: The University of Chicago Press.

Ogden, J. 1969. Mono-, bi-, and polysexuality. *Ladder* 9/10: 32-34.

O'Neil, N., and G. O'Neil. 1968. *Open Marriage.* New York: Avon Books.

Orgel, S. Z. 1957. The problem of bisexuality as reflected in circumcision. *Journal of Hillside Hospital* 5: 375-383.

Orlando [pseud.] 1978. Bisexuality — A choice not an echo? *Ms. Magazine.* Oct.
  *One of the few positive mainstream articles. A "very personal confession" from a bisexual woman.

Palm, R. 1957. A note on the bisexual origin of man. *Psychoanalysis* 5: 77-82.

Parker, E. 1968. *Spanish Fly.* Los Angeles: Echelon.

Parker, M. 1973. *The two-way swingers.* California: Barclay House.

Patry, F.L. 1928. Theories of bisexuality with report of a case. *Psychoanalytic Review* 15: 417-439.

Paul, J.P. 1984. The bisexual identity: An idea without social recognition. *Journal of Homosexuality* 9(2-3): 45-63.

————1985. Bisexuality: Reassessing our paradigms of sexuality. *Journal of Homosexuality* 11(1-2): 21-34.

Paul, J.P., and M. Rubenstein. 1988. Bisexuality: Part of who we are. *The Gaybook San Francisco,* Mar., 21-22.

Pearson, C.L. 1986. *Goodbye, I love you.* New York: Random House.

Peck, Claude. 1987. Straight and gay: Bisexualism in the twin cities. *Minneapolis-Saint Paul Magazine.* Mar., 62.

Perritte, R. 1969. *Casebook: Bisexual.*

Philipp, E. 1968. Homosexuality as seen in a New Zealand city practice. *New Zealand Medical Journal* 67: 397-401.

Philips, W.B. 1969. *The fourth sex: Bisexual.* Chatsworth, CA: Barclay House.

Playboy Readers Sex Survey. 1983. *Playboy Magazine.* May.

Pudor, H. 1906. *Bisexualität.* Berlin.

Rado, S. 1956 and 1962. *Psychoanalysis of behavior.* New York: Grune.
  *Also in *Sexual inversion,* ed. J. Marmor, 175-189. New York: Basic Books (1965). (Originally appeared in *Psychoanalytic Medicine* 2(1940): 459-467.)
  *For 25 years this negative critique of the concept of bisexuality was the most frequently cited piece in the journal literature, at a time when Stekel's inconclusive work (see separate listing) was the most frequently cited book. An alternative literature began to develop only in the late 1960s.

Randolph, L.B. 1988. The hidden fear: Black women, bisexuals, and the AIDS risk. *Ebony*, Jan.

*Aimed at a black audience, this article portrays bisexual men as secretive, double-faced, and dangerous.

Rangell, L. 1963. On friendship. *Journal of the American Psychoanalytic Association* 11: 3-54.

Raven, S. 1960. Boys will be boys. *Encounter* 20: 19-24.

*On page 20, in discussing a young British guardsman who sells sexual favors and who denies that is at all "queer," Raven asserts that "he is, in fact, bisexual," and briefly supports this position.

Reiss, E. 1986. *The aesthetic realism of Eli Siegel and the change from homosexuality*. New York: Definition Press.

Richardson, F. 1972. *Napoleon: Bisexual emperor*. New York: Horizon Press.

Richmond, L., and G. Noguera, eds. 1973. *The gay liberation book*. San Francisco: Ramparts Press.

Roazen, P. 1969. *Brother animal: The story of Freud and Tausk*. New York: Knopf.
*See especially the section "Plagiarism," on the Fleiss-Weininger affairs. Kurt Eissler (see separate listing) wrote a book to refute Roazen's book.

Robbins, B. 1967. *The fourth sex*. Canoga Park, CA: Viceroy Books.

Robertiello, R.C. 1978. The "fag hag." *Journal of Contemporary Psychotherapy* 10: 10-11.

*Discusses women who sought out lovers who were homosexual, bisexual or extremely passive men.

Rochlin, G. 1980. *The masculine dilemma: A psychology of masculinity*. Boston: Little, Brown.

Roessler, T., and R.W. Deisher. 1972. Youthful male homosexuality. *Journal of the American Medical Association* 219: 1018-1023.

Rogers, C. 1967. *Impulsive bi-sexuality*. Buffalo: Unique Books.

Rohrbaugh, J.F. 1979. *Women: Psychology's puzzle*. New York: Basic Books.

Rokeach, M. 1964. *The three Christs of Ypsilanti*. New York: Knopf.

Rosen, I. 1964. *The pathology and treatment of sexual deviation*. London: Oxford University Press.

Rosenberger, J.B. 1970. *Men and women who go both ways*. Los Angeles: Media Books.

Ross, H.L. 1971. Modes of adjustment of married homosexuals. *Social Problems* 18: 385-393.

Ross, M. 1979. Bisexuality: Fact or fallacy? *British Journal of Sexual Medicine* 6: 49-50.

Ross, M.W. 1984. Beyond the biological model: New directions in bisexual and homosexual research. *Journal of Homosexuality* 10(3-4): 63-70. *Argues against gender being the critical determinant of sexual relations and the essentiality of sexual "orientation."

Rosenzwieg, S. 1973. Human sexual autonomy as an evolutionary attainment, anticipating proceptive sex choice and idiodynamic bisexuality. In *Contemporary sexual behavior*, ed. J. Zubin and J. Money, 189-230. Baltimore: Johns Hopkins University Press.

Roy, D., and J. Rustum. 1972. Is monogamy outdated? In *Intimate life styles*, ed. J. DeLora and J. DeLora, Pacific Palisades, CA: Goodyear Publishing.

Rubenstein, M. 1982. An in-depth study of bisexuality and its relation to self-esteem. Doctoral diss., Institute for Advanced Study of Human Sexuality, San Francisco, CA.

Rubenstein, M., and C.A. Slater. 1985. A profile of the San Francisco Bisexual Center. *Journal of Homosexuality* 11(1-2): 227-230.

Rubin, I. 1961. *The third sex*. New York: New Book.

Rurtenbeek, H.M. 1970. *Sexuality and identity*. New York: Delta.

Rurtenbeek, H.M., ed. 1973. *Homosexuality: A changing picture*. London: Souvenir.

Russ, J. 1975. *The female man*. New York: Bantam Books.

Saliba, P. 1982. Research project on sexual orientation. *The Bi-Monthly Newsletter of the Bisexual Center of San Francisco* 6(5): 3-6.

Salzman, L. 1980. Latent homosexuality. In *Homosexual behavior*, ed.J. Marmor, 312-324. New York: Basic Books.

Sarlin, L. 1963. Feminine identity. *Journal of the American Psychoanalytic Association* 11: 790-816.

Saul, L. 1951. Wood as a bisexual symbol. *Psychoanalytic Quarterly* 20: 616.

Sawyer, E. 1965. A study of a public lesbian community. Paper presented to the Sociology-Anthropology Department of George Washington University, Washington, D.C. Available at the Alfred Kinsey Institute, Bloomington, IN.

Schaefer, S., S. Evans, and E. Coleman. 1987. Sexual orientation concerns among chemically dependent individuals. *Journal of Chemical Dependency Treatment* 1(1): 121-140.

Schafer, S. 1975. Sexuelle und soziale Probleme von Lesbierinnen in der DBR (Sexual and social problems among lesbians in the German Democratic Republic). In *Ergebnisse zur sexual Forschung*, ed. E. Schorsch and G. Schmidt, 299-325. Köln: Wissenschafts-Verlag.

———— 1977. Sociosexual behavior in male and female homosexuals: A study in sex differences. *Archives of Sexual Behavior* 6: 355-364.

Schecter, D.E. 1968. Identification and individuation. *Journal of the American Psychoanalytic Association* 16: 48-80.

Schuster, D. 1969. Bisexuality, and body as phallus. *Psychoanalytic Quarterly* 38: 72-80.

Schwartz, P., and P.W. Blumstein. 1976. Bisexuals: When love speaks louder than labels. *Ms. Magazine.* Nov., 80-81.

Scott, J. [pseud.]. 1978. *Wives who love women.* New York: Walker.

Severn, B. 1970. *Intersexuality: The bisexual male.*
  *Case histories.

Shuster, R. 1987. Sexuality as a continuum: The bisexual identity. In *Lesbian psychologies: Explorations and challenges,* ed. Boston Lesbian Psychologists Collective. Champaign, IL: University of Illinois Press.

Sides, W.H. 1986. Of lovers and their friends. *Washingtonian.* Nov., 127.

Simeon, A.T.W. 1961. *Man's presumptuous brain.* New York: Dutton.

Singer, J. 1977. *Androgyny: Toward a new theory of sexuality.* New York: Doubleday.

Sinha, J.B. 1986. The Mahatma: Tougher than thunder and softer than flowers. *Dynamische Psychiatrie* 19(6): (101) 507-515.
  *Discusses Mahatma Gandhi's bisexuality and androgyny in both his public and private lives.

Sisley, E.L., and B. Harris. 1977. *The joy of lesbian sex.* New York: Crown.

Smith, D.C. 1981. *The naked child: The long-range effects of family and social nudity.* Saratoga, CA: R. and E. Publishers.

Smith-Rosenberg, C. 1975. The female world of love and ritual: Relations between women in nineteenth century America. *Signs: Journal of Women in Culture and Society* 1(1): 1-29.

Socarides, C.W. 1963. The historical development of theoretical and clinical concepts of overt female homosexuality. *Journal of the American Psychoanalytic Association* 11: 385-414.

———— 1968. Homosexuality in the male: A report of a psychiatric study group. *International Journal of Psychiatry* 11: 460-469.

———— 1968. *The overt homosexual.* New York: Grune & Stratton.

Sours, J.A. 1974. Growth and development in childhood. In *American handbook of psychiatry,* Vol. 1, ed. A. Arieti. New York: Basic Books.

Spada, J. 1979. *The Spada report.* New York: New American Library.

Sperling, M. 1971. Spider phobias and spider fantasies: A clinical contribution to the study of symbol and symptom choice. *Journal of the American Psychoanalytic Association* 19: 472-498.

Spiers, D.E. 1976. The no-man's land of the bisexual. *Psychiatry* 22(3): 6-11.

Spruiell, V. 1978. Groddeck's children. *Journal of the Philadelphia Association for Psychoanalysis* 6: 175-181.

Starkweather, D. 1974. Bisexuality is not succotash. *Village Voice*, Aug. 15, 27.

Staver, S. 1987. Bisexual spreads HIV to family: Extent of transmission unclear. *American Medical News*.Sep. 4, 3.

Stearn, J. 1962. *The sixth man*. Philadelphia: McFadden.

Stekel, W. 1944. *Bi-Sexual love*. New York: Emerson Books; Miami, FL: Brown Books (1950).

Stimpson, C. 1974. The androgyne and the homosexual. *Women's Studies* 2: 237-247.

Stokes, K., P.R. Kilmann, and R.L. Wanlass. 1983. Sexual orientation and sex role conformity. *Archives of Sexual Behavior* 12(5): 427-433.

Stoller, R.J. 1972. The bedrock of masculinity and femininity: Bisexuality. *Archives of General Psychiatry* 26: 207-212.

―――― 1980. A different view of Oedipal conflict. In *The course of life*, Vol. 1, ed. S. Greenspan and G. Pollock, 589-602.

―――― 1974. Facts and fancies: An examination of Freud's concept of bisexuality. In *Women and analysis*, ed. J. Strouse, 343-364. New York: Viking.

―――― 1973. The impact of new advances in sex research on psychoanalytic theory. *American Journal of Psychiatry* 130: 241-251.

―――― 1975. *Perversion: The erotic form of hatred*. New York: Pantheon.

―――― 1976. Primary femininity. *Journal of the American Psychoanalytic Association* (supplement) 24: 59-78.

―――― 1968. *Sex and gender: On the development of masculinity and femininity*, Vol. 1. New York: Aronson.

―――― 1979. *Sexual excitement: Dynamics of erotic life*. New York: Pantheon.

―――― 1973. *Splitting: A case of female masculinity*. New York: Quadrangle.

Stoller, R.J., and L.E. Newman. 1971. The bisexual identity of transsexuals: Two case examples. *Archives of Sexual Behavior* 1: 17-28.

Stone, L. L. 1981. Women who live with gay men. *Ms. Magazine*, Oct. 103-104.

Storms, M.D. 1980. Theories of sexual orientation. *Journal of Personality and Social Psychology* 38(5): 783-792.

Strutt, M. 1970. *Bisexual swapping*. Chatsworth, CA: Barclay House.

Sulloway, F.J. 1979. *Freud, biologist of the mind: Beyond the psychoanalytic legend*. New York: Basic Books.

*Extremely informative on the Freud/Fliess controversy and has an excellent presentation of early theorizing on bisexuality in the late 1800s.

Summer, W. 1955. On the bisexuality of man. *Mattachine Review*. Jul./Aug., 16-18.

Suppe, F. 1984. In defense of a multidimensional approach to sexual identity. *Journal of Homosexuality* 10(3-4): 7-14.
*Discusses Shively and De Cecco's model for components of sexual identity.

Talbot, D. 1986. Unspeakable pleasures: Erotic adventures in the 80s. *New Age*, Feb., 27.

Thornton, N. 1948. Why American homosexuals marry. *Neurotica* 1(1): 24-28.

Tripp, C.A. 1976. *The homosexual matrix*. New York: McGraw-Hill.

Vail, A. 1963. *My bisexual three years*. Chicago: Novel Books.
*As told to Con Sellers.

Valaverde, M. 1985. *Sex power and pleasure*. Canada: The Women's Press.
*Chapter 4: "Bisexuality: Coping with sexual boundaries."

Van-Wyck, P.H. 1984. A critique of Dorner's analysis of hormonal data from bisexual males. *Journal of Sex Research* 20(4): 412-414.
*Criticizes prenatal hormonization as a basis for sexual orientation.

Van-Wyck, P.H., and C.S. Geist. 1984. Psychosocial development of heterosexual, bisexual, and homosexual behavior. *Archives of Sexual Behavior* 13(6): 505-544.

Vassi, M. 1975. *Metasex, myth and madness*. New York: Penthouse Press.

Vidal, G. 1973. Bisexual politics. In *The gay liberation book*, ed. L. Richmond and G. Noguera, 134-137. San Francisco: Ramparts Press.

Vorhaus, M. 1959. *Adam's rib: An analysis of normal bisexuality in each of us*. New York: Horizon Press.

Warren, C.A.B. 1974. *Identity and community in the gay world*. New York: John Wiley & Sons.

Wayson, P.D. 1985. Personality variables in males as they relate to differences in sexual orientation. *Journal of Homosexuality* 11(1-2): 63-73.
*A study of 114 white males which determined that heterosexuals are more competitive, and that bisexuals have greater difficulty focusing their attention in a disciplined way.

Weinberg, G. 1972. *Society and the healthy homosexual*. New York: St. Martin's Press.

Weinberg, M.S., and C.J. Williams. 1974. *Male homosexuals: Their problems and adaptations*. New York: Oxford University Press.

Weinberg, T.S. 1977. On "doing" and "being" gay: Sexual behavior and homosexual self-identity. Paper presented at the annual meeting of the Society for the Study of Social Problems, Alfred C. Kinsey Institute, Bloomington, IN.

Weininger, O. n.d. *Sex and character* 6th ed. London: Heinemann; New York: Putnam's.

*First edition published as Geschlecht und Charakter, Vienna, 1903.

Weinrich, J.D. 1988. The periodic table model of the gender transpositions: Limerent and lusty sexual attractions and the nature of bisexuality. *Journal of Sex Research* 24: 113-129.

Weiss, E. 1958. Bisexuality and ego structure. *International Journal of Psychoanalysis* 39: 91-97.

Weissman, P. 1962. Structural considerations in overt male bisexuality. *International Journal of Psychoanalysis* 42: 159-168.

West, D.J. 1977. *Homosexuality re-examined.* Minneapolis: University of Minnesota Press.

Westwood, G. 1960. *A minority — A report on the life of the male homosexual in Great Britain.* London: Longmans, Green.

Willis, D. 1974. Bisexuality: A personal view. *Women: A Journal of Liberation* 4(1): 10.

Wise, D. 1971. *Understanding bisexuality.* Los Angeles: Centurion Press.

Wise, D., and J. Jardine. 1971. *The bisexual male.* Los Angeles: Centurion Press.

Wittels, F. 1929. *Critique of love.* New York: Macaulay.

——— 1954. Heinrich von Kleist: A Prussian Junker and creative genius: A study in bisexuality. *American Imago* 11: 11-31.

——— 1954. Mona Lisa and feminine beauty: A study in bisexuality. *International Journal of Psychoanalysis* 15: 25-40.

——— 1934. Motherhood and bisexuality. *Psychoanalytic Review* 21: 180-193.

Wolf, T.J. 1987. Group counseling for bisexual men. *Journal for Specialists in Group Work* 12(4): 162-165.

——— 1987. Group psychotherapy for bisexual men and their wives. *Journal of Homosexuality* 14(1-2): 191-199.

——— 1985. Marriages of bisexual men. *Journal of Homosexuality* 11(1-2): 135-148.

*An examination of 26 heterosexually married couples in which the husband was bisexual.

——— 1982. Selected social and psychological aspects of male homosexual behavior in marriage. Doctoral diss., United States International University, San Diego, CA.

Wolfe, C. 1977. *Bisexuality: A study.* London: Quartet Books.

Wolfenden, J. 1957. *Report on the committee on homosexual offenses and prostitution.* London: H.M. Stationery Office.

Wolman, B., ed. 1977. *International encyclopedia of psychiatry, psychology and psychoanalysis.* New York: Van Nostrand Reinhold.

Wooden, W., and J. Parker. 1982. *Men behind bars: Sexual exploitation in prison.* New York and London: Plenum Press.

Woods, M.Z. 1988. Bisexual conflict in the analysis of an adolescent boy. *Journal of Child Psychotherapy* 14(1): 33-49.

Wright, L.S., and S. Fling. 1983. Perceptions of self and parents among college students of different sexual orientations. Paper presented at the Annual Convention of the Southwestern Psychological Association, San Antonio, Texas.

Wyckoff, H. 1973. In behalf of bisexuality. *Issues in Radical Therapy* 1(3): 10-13. *Also appears in *Love therapy and politics,* ed. H. Wyloff, 1976, Grove Press.

Wysor, B. 1974. *The lesbian myth.* New York: Random House.

Yankelovich, D. 1981. New rules in American life: Searching for self-fulfillment in a world turned upside down. *Psychology Today,* Apr., 67-75.

Zinik, G. 1985. Identity conflict or adaptive flexibility? Bisexuality reconsidered. *Journal of Homosexuality* 11(1-2): 7-19.

——— 1983. *The sexual orientation inventory.* Manuscript. University of California, Santa Barbara, CA.

Zolla, E. 1981. *The androgyne: The creative tension of male and female.* New York: Crossroad Publishing.

Zoltano, R.F. 1989. *Sex and bisexuality: Index of modern information.* Virginia: ABBE Publishers Association.

A Brief Listing of Films and Plays
From Around the Globe
Dealing with Bisexuality

These listings are by no means exhaustive; the bisexual influence in the arts is so great that it would require the work of a lifetime and many books the size of this one to even *begin* to show how bisexuality (or "the bisexual potential") is the impetus behind many great and familiar works.

What is given here, instead, is a sample of some of the films and plays from around the world that more specifically deal with bisexuality, either in their storylines or their characters.

Many thanks to Bill Himelhoch for his assistance in preparing this list.

Films

Argentina
Adios, Roberto
(Director: Enrique Dawi.) A recently divorced man is confronted with the choice of returning to his wife and son or staying with the man who has unexpectedly come into his life.

Canada
Anne Trister
(Director: Lea Pool.) Compelled by the need to create a new sense of reality, Anne leaves her male lover, moves to another city, and becomes emotionally obsessed with an older woman.

The Fox
(Director: Mark Rydell. From the novella by D.H. Lawrence.) Anne Heywood plays a woman running a farm with her female lover who is courted by a man who eventually marries her after her lover's death. Judith Crist, in her review of the movie, described the Heywood character as ". . . torn by the bisexuality that obsesses us all."

England
Butley
(Director: Harold Pinter. From the play by Simon Gray.) The story of a university professor (played by Alan Bates) who, in the course of one day, discovers that his wife and male lover are both leaving him for other men.

Sunday Bloody Sunday
(Director: John Schlesinger. With Peter Finch and Murray Head.) A young designer (male) is involved in simultaneous relationships with a doctor (male) and an executive (female). This film featured one of the first mouth-to-mouth male kisses in screen history.

France
Les Enfants Terribles (The Strange Ones)
(Director: Jean Cocteau (from his play).) The ill-fated hero is infatuated during adolescence with a boy and later falls in love with a woman who resembles the boy. (The boy and the woman are played by the same actress).

Ménage
(Director: Bertrand Blier. With Gerard Depardieu, Miou-Miou, and Michel Blanc.) The story is somewhat similar to the American films *Down and Out in Beverly Hills* or *Eating Raoul*: a free-living bisexual (played by Gerard Depardieu) "corrupts" a married couple (Miou-Miou and Michael Blanc) into all sorts of nonconformist mischief, including "unanticipated sexual practices." A review in the Cambridge (Massachussetts) *Chronicle* called it " comically subversive, sexually uninhibited" and "one of the highlights of the film year."

Italy
Al di la' del Bene e del Male (Beyond Good and Evil)
(Director: Liliani Cavani.) As an act of emancipation, Lou Andreas-Salome involves herself in a *menage à trois* with Friedrich Nietzsche and Paul Reé (who discovers his attraction to men).

Morte a Venezia (Death in Venice)
(Director: Luciano Visconti. From the novella by Thomas Mann.)
A married composer visits Venice and is entranced by the beauty of a young boy.

Satyricon
(Director: Frederico Fellini.) A complex presentation of a Latin classic: two friends fight over and share male and female loves.

Teorema
(Director: Pier Paolo Pasolini). A parable about a man who visits a wealthy, upright family and proceeds to make love to every member therein: wife, husband, daughter, son, and maid. When he leaves, the family is left dramatically and absurdly changed.

Mexico
Doña Herlinda Y Su Hijo (Doña Herlinda and Her Son)
(By Jaime Hamberto Hermosillo.) Comedy about a bisexual man whose understanding mother arranges a marriage for him which includes his male lover in the household.

The Netherlands
Een Vrouw Als Eva (A Woman Like Eve)
(Director: Nouchka van Brakel.) A married woman with children falls in love with a free-spirited lesbian.

De Vierde Man (The Fourth Man)
(Director: Paul Verhoeven.) Two men are drawn together in face of a threat to their lives from a young widow who may have murdered her previous husbands.

United States of America
Advise and Consent
(Director: Otto Preminger. From the novel by Allen Drury.) A U.S. senator commits suicide when a brief closeness with another soldier during his war service is made public.

The Best Man
(Director: Franklin Schaffner. From the novel by Gore Vidal, who wrote the screenplay.) A story of political ambition.

Beyond Therapy
(Director: Robert Altman. From the play by Christopher Durang.) An openly bisexual (but eccentric) man woos and wins a resistant woman in a mileu of bizarre psychiatrists.

Cabaret
(Director: Bob Fosse. From the play *I Am a Camera* by John van Druten, from the stories by Christopher Isherwood.) Kit Kat Club singer Sally Bowles shares her male lover with a German baron.

Desert Hearts
(Director: Donna Deitch. Based on Jane Rule's novel, *Desert of the Heart*.) A college professor retreats to a Nevada ranch to arrange a Reno divorce; she falls in love with a lesbian charmer.

Dog Day Afternoon
(Director: Sidney Lumet.) True story of Littlejohn Basso, a bisexual man involved in concurrent marriages with a male and a female, who gets in over his head when he robs a bank to pay for his transsexual husband's sex-change operation.

Kiss of the Spider Woman
(Director: Hector Babenco.) Two prisoners share a cell, one a gay man arrested on morals charges and the other a straight political prisoner. At the end of the film they sleep together, as the "straight" prisoner applies his politics of equality to the two of them.

Making Love
(Director: Arthur Hiller.) A happily married young physician (played by Michael Ontkean) explores his homoerotic desires, while his wife tries to be understanding.

Five well-known actors turned down the role of the doctor

before the director finally found Michael Ontkean (Tom Berenger, Michael Douglas, Harrison Ford, William Hurt [who later went on to play the homosexual Molina in *Kiss of the Spider Woman*], and Peter Strauss all refused). According to *The Gay Book of Lists* (Leigh W. Rutledge, Alyson Publications, 1987), director Hiller said that most actors, when approached with the possibility of playing the doctor, flatly replied "Don't even think about me for this."

Mass Appeal
(From the play by Bill Davis.) A seminary student puts his vocation in jeapordy by standing up for two gay seminarians and announcing his own bisexuality.

Plays

Where there is a movie version (as is noted by an *), annotations will be found in the above section on *films*.

*The Best Man, Gore Vidal

*Beyond Therapy, Christopher Durang

*Butley, Simon Gray

*Les Enfants Terribles, Jean Cocteau

Gemini, Albert Innaurato
An Ivy-league student, having an affair with a female classmate and also attracted to her brother, is surprised when the siblings unexpectedly visit him in his Philadelphia home.

Go-See, Norris Church Mailer (unpublished: presented at Actors Studio in New York City)
A bisexual anthropologist, upon his return from studying homosexual rituals in New Guinea, is attracted to a woman who doubts

his commitment to her. He asks her to examine whether she herself "fits neatly into a slot." She admits that "once in everybody's life the lines blur."

I Am a Camera, John van Druten (from the stories by Christopher Isherwood)
Also the musical version, *Cabaret*, by Kander and Ebb, and the film of the same name.

Mass Appeal, Bill Davis, 1981

P.S. Your Cat is Dead, James Kirkwood
An out-of-work New York actor comes home to find that his girlfriend has left him, his cat is dead, and his apartment is being buglarized — again. He catches the burglar, ties him to the kitchen counter, and lets out his frustrations on him, yelling and screaming, playing mind-games with him. During the course of the play, their characters become clearer, including the burglar's healthy bisexual attitudes. By the end, they talk about moving to Mexico together, and leaving the city behind.

The Shadow Box, Michael Cristofer
Won the Tony award for best play of the 1976-1977 season and its author won the Pulitzer Prize. Part of the story concerns a heterosexually married man living with his male lover at a hospice where he is dying of cancer.

The War Widow (TV play), Harvey Perr, 1976
During World War I, a woman discovers her love for a female photographer while her husband is away, fighting.

Contributors

Albert Richard Allgeier, Ph.D., a former clinical director of the Wood County Mental Health Center in Bowling Green, Ohio, is now in private practice in that city.

Elizabeth Rice Allgeier, Ph.D. is associate professor of psychology at Bowling Green (Ohio) State University.

Bill Himelhoch, founder of the New York City Bisexual Support Group, now lives in Jamaica Plain, Massachusetts, and provides therapy and counseling services to the bisexual community of the Boston area.

Fritz Klein, M.D. now has a private practice in psychiatry in San Diego.

Gary North is an editor with a national daily newspaper chain and is editor of *Bisexuality: News, Views, and Networking*. He has been active in gay/bi/lesbian organizations since 1976. He resides in Long Beach, California.

Robyn Ochs is a founder of the Boston Bisexual Women's Network and the East Coast Bisexual Network. She lives in Cambridge, Massachusetts.

Andy Plumb lives in California.

Amanda Udis-Kessler is a musician and writer living in Somerville, Massachusetts.

Charles Steir plans to publish a comprehensive annotated bibliography on bisexuality at some time in the future. He lives in New York City.

"Vi" is one of the founders of the Manchester (England) Women's Bisexual Group.

Pamela Walker is an education specialist and video producer living in Berkeley, California.

Beth Reba Weise is a writer and the editor of *North Bi Northwest*, newsletter of the Seattle Bisexual Women's Network.

Melinda Wittstock lives in Ottawa, where she is national features writer at the Canadian University Press, a nonprofit news and features service for student newspapers.

Timothy J. Wolf, Ph.D. has a private practice in psychotherapy in San Diego.

Authorship of — or mention by name in — any part of this book should not be construed to indicate a person's sexual orientation unless it is explicitly stated by that person.

Some classics from

TIMES CHANGE PRESS

HELLO, I LOVE YOU! Voices from within the Sexual Revolution — Edited by Jeanne paslé-green and Jim Haynes. 48 pioneer participants in the pre-AIDS sexual revolution — many of them feminists and political activists — share their most intimate experiences in interviews and personal statements. At stake was a search for better ways for all of us to relate to ourselves and each other. We read of these strivings with nostalgia today, but they may alert us to future possibilities. ISBN 0-87810-032-6 *175 pp; $6.95*

THIS WOMAN: Poetry of Love and Change — Barbara O'Mary. This journal from the seventies tells of a year of intense change — involving Barbara's lovers male and female, her daughters, her job, her politics, her fears, her visions. Simple, intimate and honest poetry with which we identify immediately, as it clarifies our own experience. 2d printing. ISBN 0-87810-024-5 *Illustrated; 64pp; $3.25*

AMAZON EXPEDITION: A Lesbianfeminist Anthology — Edited by Phyllis Birkby, Bertha Harris, Jill Johnston, Esther Newton, and Jane O'Wyatt. When lesbians within the gay liberation movement synthesized gay politics with feminism, they started a separate political/cultural development with which thousands of women began to identify. Lesbianism was liberated by feminist consciousness from the closets, definitions, and lifestyles imposed by the heterosexually dominant society. And feminism was invigorated and made whole — liberated by lesbianism from the limits of making changes only in relation to men. This is what this anthology is about. Culture, herstory, politics, celebration. Lesbian/feminism — one concept: the new womanity. 3d printing. ISBN 0-87810-026-1 *Illustrated; 96 pp; $4.95* ISBN 0-87810-526-3 *Cloth, $10.95*

Available again

GREAT GAY IN THE MORNING! One Group's Approach to Communal Living and Sexual Politics — The 25 to 6 Baking & Trucking Society. Somebody said, "Time is oppressive!" and stopped the clocks at 25 to 6 — and so the commune's name was registered in the local phone book, reflecting a new way of living that had begun. This is a testimony to gay optimism in the late sixties and early seventies. ISBN 0-87810-521-2 *Illustrated; 96 pp; Cloth, $10.95*

LESSONS FROM THE DAMNED: Class struggle in the black community — by the damned. This highly praised book describes the awareness of oppression as black people, as workers and poor people under capitalism, and as women and young people oppressed by men and the family. It may be the first time that poor and petit-bourgeois black people have told their own story. Reissued 1990 with a new introduction. ISBN 0-87810-036-9 *Illustrated; viii+156 pp; $7.95*

Recent from TCP

HOW DEEP IS DEEP ECOLOGY? with an essay-review on Woman's Freedom — George Bradford. A veteran activist of social/environmental radicalism critiques some writings coming out of the deep-ecology movement and posits a close relationship between freedom for women and the salvation of the earth. ISBN 0-87810-035-0 *Illustrated; x+84 pp; $5.50*

Our Books Are Available from Quality Bookstores

To order direct, send your order and payment (including $1.50 postage and handling for the first item, 75¢ for each additional item: minimum total $5) to: Times Change Press, Publishers Services, P.O. Box 2510, Novato, CA 94948. Orders for California delivery must include local sales tax.

Prices may change. Foreign orders add 30% rounded to nearest $US; surface delivery included.